GUERRILLAS
OF
PEACE

GUERRILLAS OF PEACE

LIBERATION THEOLOGY
AND THE
CENTRAL AMERICAN REVOLUTION

toExcel
San Jose New York Lincoln Shanghai

Guerrillas of Peace
Liberation Theology and the Central American Revolution

Published by toExcel
an imprint of iUniverse.com, Inc.

For information address:
iUniverse.com, Inc.
620 North 48th Street
Suite 201
Lincoln, NE 68504-3467
www.iuniverse.com

Originally published by South End Press

ISBN: 0-595-00418-0

Printed in the United States of America

This book is dedicated to my wife, Theresa Killeen Bonpane
and to my children, Colleen Marie and Blase Martin.
Liberation has made our family possible.

Table of Contents

Introduction

Fortunately, the Church today can no longer be trusted as a stabilizing element for Central American dictatorships. Yet, coexistence with repressive regimes had been a notable characteristic of the Church ever since the days of the Roman Emperor Constantine. This conformity to repression has fostered weak and often hypocritical postures in segments of the Church.

As the institutional Church began to coexist with imperial power, it developed the following characteristics: (1) *Formalism*, a focus on worship with ritual correctness and the *ex opere operato* concept of the sacraments acting—in contrast to the *ex opero operantis* view of the subject acting. Such religious passivity can coexist nicely with repression, injustice, and fascism. In fact, the very leaders of such regimes are comfortable worshiping in such a setting. Surely no dictator would oppose praise for God and country.[1](2) *Legalism*, a legalistic emphasis on sin, where guilt is wholesaled, types and severity of sin are defined, and forgiveness is individually retailed. In a repressive regime it is opportune for the Church to remind the faithful of their guilt. (3) *Triumphalism*, absolute confidence in the perfection of one's position. Triumphalism combines with stylized worship and guilt to complete the formula for nonaction which suits precisely the needs of a repressive regime.

In this framework, service to the poor becomes an individual response to a subjective case and not a systemic response to an objective condition. The State is considered a constant, the institutional Church is considered a constant, and so is misery.[2] Individual churchpeople need not consciously select this repressive posture; longstanding tradition and training have crystalized it and given it legitimacy.

Church leadership generally adopts the material values and viewpoint of the ruling class in the repressive regime to which it conforms. Ritual participation and personal chastity become a definition of sanctity. In such a setting, neither clergy nor laity need be considered a threat.[3] While Central American clerics have generally

1

2   GUERRILLAS OF PEACE

conformed to the *de jure* State, the exceptional cases discussed in this book highlight clear trends of a different nature. For just as the institutional Church has been able to coexist with repressive regimes, so too since the early days of the Roman Empire, has a primitive, clandestine, illegal Christianity challenged the very fabric of repressive regimes and appeared as a healthy and prophetic force.[4]

From Conformity to Opposition: The Cursillos de Capacitacion Social (1962-1967)

The arrival of Pope John XXIII in 1958 took many traditional churchpeople by surprise. During his office, there was a new concern for primitive Christian values. The traditions of formalism, legalism, and triumphalism came under attack. The encyclical letters *Mater et Magistra* and *Pacem in Terris* identified the real devils as malnutrition, ignorance, and disease.[5]

The reformation of Martin Luther had little effect on the Latin American Catholic Church. But the impact of the Second Vatican Council in 1965 was cataclysmic. An enthusiastic program called Los Cursillos de Capacitación Social (Workshops on the Social Problem) was started in Venezuela. At its inception, the program—not to be confused with the Cursillos de Christianidad which were doctrinally oriented—was simply a Catholic response to alleged communist infiltration in the university. As an anticommunist movement the cursillos had the objective of Christian revolution in Latin America. The cursillos were developed throughout Central America by the Jesuits and the Maryknoll Fathers and Sisters working very closely with university and high school students. To the surprise of its founders, instead of adhering to their stated objectives, the cursillos became an effective instrument of Marxist-Christian dialogue both in study and in action.[6]

Generally, the location for the cursillo was a suburban retreat. The original atmosphere was militaristic. An iron discipline was maintained during the eight days of rigid intellectual and physical exercise. The participants, young men and women of high school and college age, were to enter into the seriousness of the program or leave the retreat. Catholic professionals or priests generally delivered the academic classes. Subjects included God and science, the Church, Christian morality, the family, modern social problems, the social doctrine of the Church, and university action.

Dictatorial regimes require anti-intellectualism and an ahistorical perspective. Illiteracy is the desired condition for the masses and its antithesis, university education and reflective thought, are identified as subversive. By 1965 thousands of the best educated citizens of Nicaragua, El Salvador, and Guatemala were being slaughtered in a vast institutional drive for political unconsciousness. It was in this atmosphere that the Cursillos de Capacitación Social were operating in Central America where (except for Costa Rica) anything and anybody to the left of the Christian Democratic Party was under attack physically.[7]

The cursillos quickly adapted to the local reality of misery, foreign economic domination, guerrilla warfare, and the direct intervention of the U.S. military.[8] Thousands of Central American participants became conscious that their goal was not to refute Marxism or to promote Christian Democracy. Their goal was to solve the Central American problem.

A new element in the Central American Church took hold as a result of Vatican II: the practice of democracy and dialogue. Titles were dropped by the members of El Centro de Capacitación Social. Everyone was compañero and compañera including priests and sisters. After many weeks as apprentices, university students were capable of giving the majority of the cursillo classes. Participants were deeply immersed in the Central American social, political, and economic reality. Cursillo themes included the following: Central American problems must be solved at the roots; existing structures fail to provide for the spiritual or material well-being of the Central American people; glaring injustices, evident in statistical studies and encountered through personal experience, make it clear that a revolution is necessary to achieve social justice; the revolution should be peaceful and legal, but if necessary it will be violent;[9] the dignity of the human person must be realized; the worker is a person and not "cheap labor"; capitalist enterprise must be opposed because of the sharp division between capital and labor, and the unilateral position taken by capital in decision making.

By 1966 cursillo leaders were saying that their objective in Central America was to create a Christian enterprise which was neither capitalist nor socialist, a society in which the profits of the owners would be shared by all the workers. The emphasis was on revolution: "We cannot Christianize capitalism with paternalistic patches. We will lose many of our privileges for the greater general betterment. There will be opposition, and armed resistance will be called for if necessary."[10]

The cursillos were brought to the rural sectors of Central America by an experienced student vanguard, together with priests and sisters who had been their mentors. They called for the expropriation of unused lands on behalf of the common good, and peasant leagues were fostered as essential to the attainment of campesino justice.[11]

A growing militancy was obvious at an international convention of Cursillos de Capacitación Social, held in Costa Rica in January of

1967. Many participants had determined that philosophical marxism had a deep rapport with Christianity. The *Populorum Progressio* encyclical of Pope Paul VI was seen as having a series of marxist derivations. Papal opposition to violent revolution was stated in this new encyclical with such clear qualification in section 31 that many Central Americans considered the qualification to be a mandate in support of their liberation armies:

> We know, however, that a revolutionary uprising—*save where there is manifest, longstanding tyranny which would do great damage to fundamental personal rights and dangerous harm to the common good of the country*—produces new injustices, throws more elements out of balance and brings on new disasters. [Italics added]

Central American members of the cursillos were also delighted with section 81 of the same encyclical letter:

> It belongs to laymen, without waiting passively for orders and directives, to take the initiative freely and infuse a Christian spirit into the mentality, customs, laws and structures of the community in which they live.

Encouraged by what they considered a new papal directive, cursillo leaders made changes in their programs. Six-week literacy training programs and day-long programs on hygiene were developed, and meetings with peasants interested in forming leagues were organized. This increased exposure to the rural population led to a better understanding of the guerrilla position. By 1967 armed rebels would appear unannounced at cursillo programs. They would speak privately and informally with participants and occasionally they would address the entire group. They often expressed admiration for the cursillo system but warned that as the movement grew it would be stopped. They urged the students to understand the importance of armed resistance. The combination of academic background and courage of the guerrilla leadership left the students with a sense of respect and admiration.[12]

In 1967 the cursillos were stopped by the Cardinal Archbishop of Guatemala. Journalists from the United States began investigative coverage of the Centro de Capacitación Social. News of "the Guerrillas of Peace" spread throughout the United States and Latin America, and many journalists correctly reported the mission of the Cursillos de Capacitación Social as one of the last effective nonviolent programs in Central America. David Mangurian and Vern Richey, writing for the Copley News Service, claimed that the students and their leaders were very apt to enter the armed struggle if their program was stopped. Their analysis was correct, but the articles had the negative effect of attracting the government's attention. As the reporting made clear, the cursillos represented a dynamic instrument of social and political awareness. An unprecedented integration was taking place between urban students and Indian peasants; between marxist humanists and Christian humanists.[13] As a result of this growth in awareness among concerned youth, the Central American Church would never be the same again.

The flurry of publicity, organizing, and opposition in the midst of daily shootings and bombings was more than Archbishop Mario Casariego, Metropolitan of Central America, could tolerate. He ordered the national adviser to the cursillos to "tell the students to stay out of politics!" Student reaction to the mandate to stay out of politics was immediate and unanimous. The Centro de Capacitación Social declared itself thereafter to be a secular organization, independent of the hierarchy of the Catholic Church. The students insisted that it was the business of laypeople to enter into politics. The Archbishop did not take further action at the time since he feared that if the Church totally alienated the students, the Centro would take the dangerous step of becoming a clandestine organization. Such fears were not unfounded.

Observing the crisis in the cursillos, leaders of the guerrilla organization Fuerzas Armadas Rebeldes (FAR or Armed Rebel Forces) approached Centro members with a proposal for the leadership of both organizations to meet and discuss the future of Central American revolution. At a farmhouse near Esquintla, members of FAR and the cursillos reached a consensus that a new group to be called the Christian Revolutionary Front could bring different strata and classes of Central America together. Such a front would in no way oppose existing guerrilla groups but it would extend the revolutionary call to the Christian Indian community. At this point Cursillos de Capacitación Social left behind its past as an anti-communist Catholic program and became an integrated movement of social and political revolution.[14]

To no one's surprise, the change in the Cursillos de Capacitación Social did not go unnoticed by ruling elites—secular and religious. Ecclesiastical superiors informed the U.S. Ambassador in Guatemala, and names of all leaders were reported to the secret police. The Ambassador ordered immediate expulsion of U.S. missionaries working with the Christian Revolutionary Front "because they would not be protected." After months of clandestine training, study, and reflection in Mexico, the Christian Revolutionary Front disbanded. All involved determined to enter the ranks of existing revolutionary movements or to seek other avenues to express their dedication.

The Cursillos de Capacitación Social were a major factor in the politicization of the Central American clergy. They provided an experience of a disciplined movement in communion with the people[15] which led to a rapid raising of social and political consciousness.[16]

"Communist" clergy were branded as the enemy in El Salvador, Honduras, and Guatemala. Many church people were arrested and some were executed in the struggle for justice. But the Church of Liberation would not be turned back.

The 1968 Latin American Bishops Conference at Medellin in Colombia lent strong support to the priests and religious supporting revolutionary change in Central America. Among those already deeply involved was Father Ernesto Cardenal, one of Latin America's best known poets, who under the Somoza dictatorship organized the community of Solentiname on an island in the Lake of Nicaragua. The Gospel in Solentiname was primitive, clear, and revolutionary. Worried by its inspiring example, Somoza sent the National Guard to the island in 1978 and destroyed the community. Father Cardenal, currently Minister of Culture in the Nicaraguan government, responded with the following message:

> The government of Nicaragua has accused me of illicit association with the National Liberation Front of Sandino [FSLN]. Now is the moment in which I declare publicly that I do belong to the FSLN and this is an honor.
>
> I consider it my duty as a poet and as a priest to belong to this movement. In these Latin American countries which are fighting for their liberation, the poet cannot be alien to the struggle of the people and much less can a priest.
>
> I belong to the FSLN above all because of my fidelity to the gospel. It is because I want a radical and profound change, a new and fraternal society in accord with the teaching of the gospels. It is because I consider this a priestly struggle...[17]

Toward a New Coexistence: Christianity and Revolution

Clearly, in the contemporary Central American reality, marxism has had a profound impact on the Church and Christianity has had a profound impact on marxism. The 1959 Cuban revolution had an irreversible impact on the Central American Church. Its ability to cast out the true devils of illiteracy, disease, and hunger has been witnessed internationally. Speaking to Catholics about the Cuban revolution in 1971, Fidel Castro observed:

> We have now arrived at the point not simply of coexistence between religion and revolution but for the best possible relationship. A Christian who understands Christ's words in their essence simply cannot be on the side of the exploit-

ers, on the side of those who promote injustice, hunger and misery.

I always admired and deeply appreciated those Little Sisters who went to work with lepers at various institutions because they signified an enlightenment, a capacity to sacrifice for others. Persons doing this dangerous, selfless work are practicing ideal communist conduct!

In recent times within the very bosom of Christian movements, there have arisen revolutionary currents, progressive currents which are escalating into revolutionary positions and there are a great number of priests and religious who hold a firm position in favor of the process of liberation of Latin America.[18]

The popularity of Karl Marx and *The Communist Manifesto* demanded an answer from the Church. Official answers began with *Rerum Novarum* of Pope Leo XIII. Forty years later, Pius XI made further commentary on the question with *Quadragesimo Anno*. In spite of disciplinary action against Catholics who joined the communist parties, and in spite of many apparently contradictory positions regarding their support of capital, the social-political-economic observations in the papal documents of the last century were responsive to the overpowering influence of marxism.

The very diagnosis of society formulated in the 19th Century by Pope Leo XIII and developed thereafter by his successors, is a marxian diagnosis. Society is seen as divided into classes in which there are owners of the means of production and others, the workers, able only to contribute their labor and forced to submit to the decision making power of the capitalists. The confrontation between these two classes and the inevitability of conflict is affirmed in *Quadragesimo Anno*. What Pius XI calls "confrontation," Marx calls "struggle." What Marx calls a classless society, the pontiff calls a "society free of classes."

It does not seem realistic to discuss whether or not there is class struggle any more than it is realistic to discuss whether or not there is violence. Class struggle is a reality. Every time a worker in El Salvador or elsewhere receives ten dollars for a month of labor we know there is class struggle in fact. The wealthy will unjustly struggle to maintain their control. Their tools include torture and murder. People do not promote class struggle or violence as some sort of good. On the contrary, they confront class struggle and violence as evils that must be dealt with openly, as societal diseases. Class struggle will be eliminated when there is fairness in the distribution of goods and services. And most societal violence will disappear as a byproduct of this new fairness. The State will indeed "wither away" as we know it when people are truly participating in social, economic, and political decisions.

Unfortunately, we have been brought up on parlor games, where the participants discuss whether or not they are "for" or "against" violence. Can you picture a similar discussion on whether we are for or against disease. Violence, class struggle, and disease are all real. They do not go away through mystification. Anyone who loves violence, disease, or class struggle is some kind of a nut. But those who deny the reality of violence and class struggle—like those who would deny the reality of disease—are not dealing with the real world.

Injustice piled up from generation to generation has finally achieved its near perfect systematic institutionalization. In liberation theology, therefore, the struggle is to see that the destruction of capitalism includes the destruction of all injustice. The fetishization of labor as an object was denounced by Marx as the very axis of the capitalist social system. Labor must become the subject.

Hatred is not part of the liberating program. Personal hatreds are for those who lack the consciousness of a way out. The poor working for revolution are doing the rich a favor. We hate the sin and not the sinner. We are fighting to restructure a system; not to punish its victims. We happen to believe that love can be systematized.

In the growing dialogue between Christianity and marxism, ecclesiastical voices of despair over the horrors of godless communism have been drowned out by the necessity of condemning godless capitalism. The challenge of this dialectic is not simply for Catholics. All of the world's religious are now divided, with those who believe that *knowing God is doing justice* on the one side, and those who are using formalism, legalism, and triumphalism as a cloak for obscurantism, on the other. The two approaches have nothing in common. The former approach is called liberation theology and can be applied to Judaism, Christianity, Islam, Buddhism or any other theological structure.

The impact of marxism on Latin American Catholicism has unleashed an irreversible dynamic. But the Church cannot be called marxist any more than Marx himself wanted to be called a marxist. He would not ask us to look back at his words alone, but to look ahead to greater insights. He was a Socrates so threatening that hemlock has been prescribed for all of his students.

Enemies of justice are uncomfortable with the Church's awakening to the needs of the poor and exploited masses. Pope John Paul II was under great pressure to condemn liberation theology at the January 1979 Conference of Latin American Bishops (CELAM) in Puebla, Mexico. Archbishop Alfonso Lopez Trujillo (later Cardinal), Secretary General of the Conference, made a successful effort to keep most liberation theologians out of the sessions. But to the surprise of many observers, there was no condemnation of marxist analysis. Instead, the Puebla Conference condemned unrestrained capitalism and military police states.

As the Puebla Conference was taking place, the Church in El Salvador faced heightened persecution. Archbishop Oscar Arnulfo Romero buried six of his brother priests, all of them cut down by right-wing hit squads in league with the government and the oligarchy. Just prior to the murder of Archbishop Romero on March 24, 1980, the Catholic clergy of El Salvador issued a statement expressing solidarity with the prelate and the Puebla Conference. The Salvadoran clergy spoke of its "preferential option for the poor":

> The Church cannot avoid persecution when it is faithful to this option; Christ was accused before Pilate because, "he stirs up the people, teaching throughout all Judea" (Luke, 23). He who heeded and preached to the poor, went about doing good, had compassion on the multitudes and did miracles to benefit the poor, was crucified because he caused disturbances by pointing out sin, injustice and violence in the nation.[19]

Within the Church hierarchy, the "preferential option for the poor" only extends so far. To take a well known example, Archbishop (now Cardinal) Miguel Obando y Bravo of Managua allowed his episcopal office to be used as a center for the Broad Front of Opposition during the revolutionary struggle in Nicaragua. After the triumph of the revolution in 1979, the Archbishop issued a pastoral letter entitled "A Christian Obligation for a New Nicaragua" in which he stated:

> If socialism means, as it should, that the interests of the majority of Nicaraguans are paramount and if it includes a model of an economic system planned with national interests in mind, that is in solidarity with and provides for increased participation by the people, we have no objections. Any social program that guarantees to use the country's wealth and resources for the common good, and that improves the quality of human life by satisfying the basic needs of all the people, seems to us to be a just program.

Although there has been a measurable improvement in nutrition, health care, and other basic needs for Nicaraguans, Cardinal Obando y Bravo is now an opponent of the Sandinista revolution as are most members of the Nicaraguan hierarchy. On a recent trip to Nicaragua, our delegates questioned the Nicaraguan Jesuits on the shift in Cardinal Obando y Bravo's position. Their response was blunt: "When the rich were opposed to Somoza, the Cardinal opposed Somoza. Now that the rich are opposed to the Sandinistas, the Cardinal opposes the Sandinistas."

A theology is coming out of Central America which will cure the errors of centuries of clericalism. As the pursuit of justice becomes the focal point, the concern for ritual correctness fades. The Church is becoming more ecumenical and more bent on service to the poor. Multitudes of the faithful including sisters, brothers, priests, and bishops are dedicated to the creativity of the followers of Cesar Sandino and to the Church as a democratic community from the base up. As I reflected in 1966:

> I believe that there always have been people working for justice. But now the situation is distinct. Now groups are forming everywhere, small communities which announce the kingdom of God.
>
> I am overwhelmed to see how these groups are so enormously similar even without having known each other.[20]

A confrontation with the Pope was not unexpected in such a dialogical and democratic environment. I sent the following letter to Pope John Paul II after his visit to Nicaragua. It was widely published in the U.S., Europe and Latin America.

Open Letter to Pope John Paul II—March, 1983

Your Holiness:

I wish to address you today in the same spirit that St. Anthony of Padua addressed his bishop saying, "I am speaking to you with the mitre on!"

You have just completed a trip to Central America. It was a bold and courageous venture, and I am certain of your good intentions. It was obvious, however, that you are isolated and severely misinformed on the dynamics of the area. Poor advice has separated you from the people of God and the march of history. As a result, you have contributed heartily to the destabilization of Nicaragua and the further advance of United States intervention in Central America.

You visited a family in mourning. That family is called Nicaragua. Some twenty of the finest of Nicaragua's youth had just been murdered by an invasion force which was trained and paid for by the United States. You walked into the home of the deceased, you ignored the bodies in front of you and to the scandal of the faithful, you publicly chastised a prominent hero of the Sandinista revolution, Father Ernesto Cardenal. History will not forget your attack on one of Latin America's best known literary figures, on the Minister of Culture of Nicaragua, on a saintly priest, a poet and a model for the faithful.

Even were you so mistaken as to consider Father Cardenal as the prodigal son of the gospel, you might remember that Jesus spoke of a father who ran up to his son and embraced him. Contrary to the example taught by Jesus, you publicly chastised this holy man and you publicly embarassed him in front of the Nicaraguan people. You were wrong to do this, Your Holiness.

You did not chastise the murderer of Archbishop Romero; you honored him. You did not chastise the fanatic murderer who is head of state in Guatemala. You did not chastise any of the officials of the United States who plot, plan and carry out murder each day.

Holy Father, your conduct toward Father Ernesto Cardenal was a scandal and you owe him a public apology. He knelt at your feet to honor you and you dishonored him.

It was curious indeed to hear you oppose the concept of a Popular Church. You seem to interpret the matter as "alternative church." Are you unaware of the practice of democracy and peoples' power down through the centuries? Would you have tried to silence the faithful of Milan as they demanded the selection of Ambrose as their Bishop? They demanded, in the same way as the Nicaraguans, Popular Power. Ambrose had not been consecrated, he had not been ordained, he had not even been baptized when he was chosen by the people to be their Bishop. Would you have said to the people of Milan, "Silence!"

You did not shake your finger at Cardinal Mario Casariego of Guatemala. The Prince of the Church has been comfortable with the savage Guatemalan government for many years. This Cardinal reminds us of the prelate which Michaelangelo chose to paint in hell. See the Sistine Chapel. When the Guatemalan Army denounces a priest, Cardinal Casariego denounces that priest. When the Guatemalan Army kills a priest the Cardinal is apt to question the apostolate of that priest. Again and again this scandalous prelate has said by his action, "We have no king but Caesar!"

As the senior Churchman in Central America, it was probably Casariego who gave you your information on the saint of Central America, Archbishop Oscar Arnulfo Romero. I would expect Casariego to tell you that the Archbishop was killed because he was a communist. I say this because at the time of our expulsion from Guatemala this tragic Cardinal Casariego referred to us as "communists and anti-Christs."

Were you not so misinformed about the life and death of Archbishop Romero you could not have reacted to his death with such coldness and lack of attention. Holy Father, should Jesus Christ walk the streets of El Salvador today, he would be crucified as a communist. Anyone who is truly incarnate with the poor of Central America is apt to be called a communist.

But you, Holy Father, came to Nicaragua to criticize the educational system of that government. Where was the Pope when the people of Nicaragua were illiterate? If their education would have depended on the Pope, they would still be illiterate. Their illiteracy was very political but we did not hear complaints from the Vatican about the politics of their illiteracy. Why do you choose to complain about the politics of their literacy? Where was the outcry from the Vatican as the people of Nicaragua died of polio and parasites? But we hear complaints now...now that polio has been removed from Nicaragua by new people and a new government.

Sincerely, Your Holiness, I believe your vision has been clouded by the poison of atheistic capitalism. The poor of the earth are simply not going to tolerate this institutionalized violence any longer. The Nicaraguans believe that health care is a right in a developed economy, they believe that education is a right and they also believe in the freedom of religion and the separation of Church and State.

The new person of whom St. Paul spoke now lives in Nicaragua. Father Ernesto Cardenal is such a person. Had your mind not been so poisoned by misinformation about him you could have learned more about this person. This new person does not make distinctions between male or female, Jew or Greek. This new person does not worship the gods of money and power. This new person sees the whole human race as family, loves all children as one's own and identifies with the common good of all. This new person has the discipline to turn the other cheek when slapped in the face but knows that no one has permission to be passive before the rape and murder of one's family or the diabolical presence of United States napalm, white phosphorous and genocidal helicopters. This new person, Your Holiness, makes history. History is not the prerogative of Popes and Kings. Those who are faithful to the past do not repeat the past. Those who are unfaithful to the past repeat the past with its ignorance and malice.

The new person, Your Holiness, can make a value judgement. The two sides in this conflict are not the same. One side represents the rich which Jesus said would have as much chance of getting into heaven as a camel passing through the eye of a needle. The other side represents the poor of which our Blessed mother said: "The Lord has shown the strength of his arm; he has swept away the high and mighty. The Lord has set kings down from their thrones and lifted up the humble. The Lord has satisfied the hungry, and sent the rich away with empty hands."

Your Holiness, you met the future in Nicaragua and you failed to recognize it. You were as one of the disciples on the way to Emmaus, you failed to recognize Jesus in Father Ernesto Cardenal, you failed to recognize Jesus in the Nicaraguan people. On the contrary, you insulted them and their miraculous achievements. May you now recognize them in the breaking of the bread.[21]

A Second Letter to Pope John Paul II—March 1985

Your Holiness:

"The Pope is with us," proclaims a banner of the CIA mercenaries as they begin another day of torturing and murdering Nicaraguan citizens. These killers are funded by U.S. taxpayers. One of our president's fondest hopes is to give them more money. Jesus said, "By the fruits you shall know them." Anyone of discernment can recognize the fruits of Ronald Reagan. Certainly, if these contras had asked you for permission to sanction their slaughter you would not have given it to them. You must clearly abhor what they are doing.

But tragically, your recent Latin American visit and many of your statements have served to promote the goals and objectives of such criminals and to further foster the destruction of Nicaragua.

And now we are aware of a decision under your immediate jurisdiction and for which you have a greater responsibility than the above mentioned matter. The great priests of the Nicaraguan revolution, the prophets who serve as the soul and limitless humanity of that revolution, the great examples for the youth of the Americas, the exemplars of the priesthood of the future, the teachers of orthodox Christianity for the hemisphere, these ministers of God and ministers of the people of Nicaragua have been publicly chastized and convicted by you. On this matter we cannot make excuses for your lack of culpability as we did on the matter of the contras.

The international press now refers to these great priests as "mister." Gone are their ecclesiastical titles. Unlettered journalists will even say, "They are no longer priests." While such statements are theologically incorrect, they are frequently repeated by poorly educated clerics. As it is, they are as much priests as you are and perhaps more so. They have not caused the devastation you are about to unleash.

By your action against these holy men you have done something the Inquisition was unable to do; condemn a whole nation. Your mistaken predecessors believed that error had no rights and they convicted Jews, atheists, and Protestants individually. How well Church history has defended them, saying "The Pope, the Bishops and the Grand Inquisitor did not do the killing. Killing was done by the secular authorities." We may find some excuses for the Popes of days gone by. How are you going to be excused?

The question in the new Inquisition is no longer, "Are you a Jew, a Protestant or an atheist?" The question today is, "Are you a communist?" And if you are, you will be killed not one at a time as the heretics of old. You will be killed all at once by napalm and indiscriminate bombing.

Now that you have discredited the soul of the Nicaraguan revolution you have cleared the way for the physical destruction of that country. Now the secular arm of the state can kill the heretics all together. Now clean cut Catholic boys from the United States, good boys who are opposed to birth control and who do not believe in abortion, can pour into Nicaragua and carry their banner, "The Pope is With Us," as they massacre Nicaraguan children. Those same good boys can fly the B-52s as they did in Vietnam. And just as that great imperialist Cardinal Spellman [my ordaining bishop] cheered them on as Chief of the Chaplains, you can cheer them on as well.

Are you still unaware that "communist" is a code word in Latin America? Would to God that you spent more time listening to the poor rather than bringing in your own distant agenda. "Communist" is simply a word to denigrate the needs of the poor in Latin America. When the poor attempt to organize, they are communists. Hundreds of people whom I served as a Maryknoll priest in Guatemala were murdered because they were called communists. I once asked a Death Squad leader why one of our most promising students had been selected for torture and death. "Because he is a communist," was the answer. When I asked how that was determined, I received a second answer, "We heard him say he would give his life for the poor." Jesus is a communist in Guatemala. Your lack of attention to the example of Archbishop Oscar Arnulfo Romero has left a vacuum in your understanding of this matter.

Indeed, we must end forever the Inquisitional assertion of our right to kill communists. We have no such right. The United States has no such right. I would urge you not to foster any such implications. When will you demand a halt to U.S. bombing in El Salvador?

If the actual practice of the governments of El Salvador or of Guatemala could demonstrate a small percentage of the humanity of the government of Poland, we might have some reason for concern about the insurgency taking place in those Central American nations. Poland has demonstrated to the world that it has a functional legal system. El Salvador and Guatemala have not. But your objective seems to be to protect Nicaragua from becoming like Poland. Just how many Nicaraguan children will have to be killed before you consider your work done?

Certainly it would be a mistake for me to consider you as personally culpable on all of these matters. But you are clearly being used. Many of your prelates spent much of 1984 campaigning for Ronald

Reagan. The President knows that they and the Pope are opposed to abortion. Ronald Reagan will therefore oppose abortion in his state of the union message and as a tradeoff the prelates will say nothing about Reagan's plans to destroy Nicaragua. Compliance to such a scheme would only demonstrate allegiance to capitalism and distance from Jesus.

If the *New York Times* correctly quotes you [2/7/85], you stated that you saw no need for papal diplomacy in Central America. You stated that you did not know what kind of mediation there could be. If that is the case, please listen. Sit down with the Contadora nations. Speak to the Roman Catholics who have constructed one of the world's most dynamic democracies in Nicaragua. These people have eliminated a culture of silence. They will continue to live in open dialogue with Church and State.

Instruct your churches in the United States and elsewhere to open their doors in sanctuary to people made homeless by imperialism. The finest Christians in the United States are being jailed because they have used their churches as a sanctuary. Would anyone be so theologically truncated as to believe we could honor Jesus in the Blessed Sacrament and fail to honor His presence in the poor?

Join Catholics, Protestants and Jews of the United States as we pledge our resistance to imperialism in Central America and as we state: If the United States invades, bombs, sends combat troops, or otherwise significantly escalates its intervention in Nicaragua or El Salvador, we pledge to join others to engage in acts of non-violent direct action at U.S. federal facilities, including U.S. federal buildings, military installations, congressional offices, offices of the Central Intelligence Agency, the State Department, and other appropriate places. We pledge to engage in non-violent civil disobedience in order to prevent or halt the death and destruction which such military action would cause for the people of Central America.

Please do not attempt to confine sin to a solely personal matter. The corporation was designed precisely so it would have no body to kick and no soul to cast into hell. There will be no peace in Central America until we deal with the reality of multi-national greed.

There are millions of Christians using marxist analysis as a tool for understanding societal ills. Marxism and Christianity are not the same. Neither are they incompatible. Nothing can serve the cause of empire better than to define socialism as godless. No one has to be a godless socialist. I would like to meet a godly capitalist.

Socialism is not going to go away. The world's best scholars and researchers understand that production based on need is superior to the religion of profit. Socialism will not be bombed away; neither will it depart by papal fiat.

And what are the fruits of the western ideology of "anti-communism?" Anti-communism is the ideology of organized crime, anti-communism is the ideology of the world's dictatorships, anti-communism is the ideology of the CIA and its Death Squads, and has given us the dope trade and a banking system which promotes international violence by multiplying hunger. Anti-communism has given us the mercenaries who are waving your banner.

Anti-communism has given us a cold war designed by weapons manufacturers both incapable and incompetent to trade in a peaceful market. These fiends have made billions in conspiracy with government, have savaged the world's economy, have become comfortable in an era of profit without production, have left millions of people homeless in the world's richest country and are willing to destroy the planet for profit.

The approach to what you are calling marxism does nothing other than buoy up the brutal position of the United States. There is a class struggle whether you choose to discuss it or not. When Latin American workers are paid ten dollars a month and their oppressors are still comfortable in our churches, it is obvious we are failing in our duty to denounce injustice. It appears that you wish to pacify the victims rather than to identify the criminals. If your prelates continue to live like rich men in the midst of misery, how can they ever understand the poor?

People all around the world are beginning to do the will of God on earth...as it is in heaven. They know they are called to make history. As they begin to practice democracy at the base, they no longer need to be assured of their importance; they know their importance.

Where there is charity and love, God is there. How confusing is the message of the hierarchy! An outsider would think our religion was one of: proper clerical garb, absolute authoritarianism, male dominance, power seeking, fear of democracy, inquisition, harshness, hatred of the socialist world, and promotion of corporate capital. How can such a legalistic, formalistic and triumphalistic image attract the world to the teachings of Jesus? It appears that much of what is being done is actually the antithesis of Jesus. Where is the fulfillment of the prophecy of Mary?

"He has shown the strength of his arm, he has swept away the high and mighty. He has set kings down from their thrones and lifted up the humble. He has satisfied the hungry with good things and sent the rich away with empty hands." (Luke, 1)

It seems that Mary understood the reality of class struggle. But there is clearly a theology of the ruling class. And such thinking has clouded the papacy since the days of Constantine.

Celibacy is a beautiful state. But the civil, ecclesiastical, human law of celibacy has a shabby history and no scriptural basis. Clerical garb is interesting historically but why don't we enter into this world as a leaven and not as an over-visible appendage on society. Democracy is far more attractive than authoritarianism. There was more democracy in the Church in the days of St. Ambrose than there is today.

There is just too much static thinking. I don't know of any nations interested in imitating the United States or the Soviet Union. I do know of many nations determined to have health care as an absolute right apart from the money economy; to have education as an absolute right apart from the money economy and who are determined to produce what is needed for the common good rather than for the greed of a few.

Marx is being as poorly received by you today as Aquinas was when he wrote. And there is an equal importance in understanding the spirituality of the matter. Marx does not look to *having* as the road to happiness. For him it is not what we have but what we are that is important. On this spiritual point capitalism is the most materialistic philosophy of the 19th century and marxism the least materialistic. Attacking marxism has simply become a way of diverting our attention from the needs of the poor. Similarly, long battles for legalistic celibacy and only males in Holy Orders simply divert from the demands of peace and justice. In recent times we have heard much about a preferential option for the poor. It is a mandate not an option! Was Jesus not identifying class conflict when he told the enemies of the poor to go to hell? (Matthew, 25)

A limited view of sin as solely personal surely takes pressure off the world's dictatorships. Join us and attack the sins of illiteracy, disease and hunger in a systematic manner. This is what Nicaragua is doing. And you condemn them?

Your position is as weak as the position of the papacy with Galileo. Priests in the service of the Nicaraguan government are the Galileos of 1985. "Politics" and "religion" will not remain static Aristotelian categories. Priests can teach mathematics but they should be forbidden from forming polities of peace and justice?

What might you do? Tell the priests of Nicaragua to retain their places in Church and Government. There is a long-standing tradition of priests in government in Central America; more than one hundred and fifty years of independence from Spain have been marked by clerical government service.

Sit down with the Contadora nations and give their useful peace proposals the prestige of your office. Stop the attacks on Nicaragua which you have fostered by desacralizing its priests and insulting its people. Return to Nicaragua and undo the harm you have done. Your de facto political power can stop a U.S. invasion.

Tens of thousands of priests have been severely treated by the Vatican precisely because of our dedication to peace and justice. Our hearts have been open to you but your heart has not been open to us. Clerics have been diverted from peace and justice by wasting time and effort on the cult of juridic celibacy.

Personally, I made the same decision as the Nicaraguan priests some seventeen years ago. My superiors were unaware, uninformed and unconscious of the realities of our lives in Central America just as you are today. I have thanked God daily for following the Spirit rather than militaristic mandates of distant and uninformed authority.

Picture with me your own last judgement and think of yourself as standing before the Lord saying: "Lord, I spent my whole life fighting communism and defending corporate capitalism." The response is clearly written: "Out of my presence, cursed as you are, into the eternal fire prepared for the devil and his angels! For I was hungry and you gave me nothing to eat. I was thirsty and you gave me nothing to drink. I was lonely and you never made me welcome. When I was naked you did nothing to clothe me; when I was sick and in prison you never cared about me." (Matthew, 25)

Certainly some members of your Curia would consider these words as "marxist materialism."

Save yourself from the blood of the Nicaraguan people. Go and visit your brothers and sisters who have something against thee. Indeed, it would be far better for you to resign than to be a party to an imperial massacre.

Personally, I am at your service always as a priest and Latin American specialist. Enclosed is a copy of my doctoral dissertation, "Liberation Theology and the Central American Revolution."

An Irreversible Dynamic

It is clear that the impetus toward conversion and purification of the Central American Church has come from forces outside the clergy. People eager and willing to sacrifice their lives for the poor have challenged the hierarchy and have won many over to the struggle for justice.

An irreversible dynamic has been released. It is the very catalyst of the hemispheric revolution and its potential was observed by Dr. Ernesto Che Guevara, just prior to his death in 1967, when he stated:

> Christians must definitively choose the revolution, and especially on our continent where the Christian faith is so important among the masses. When Christians begin to give an integral revolutionary witness, the Latin American

revolution will be invincible. Until now, Christians have permitted their doctrines to be manipulated by reactionaries.[22]

Currently many priests realize that their work for liberation entails the risk of provoking opposition from the institutional Church; but such was the case with Fathers Hidalgo and Morelos, the early 19th Century liberators of Mexico and Central America who are now heroes of nation and church.

Consider these words from Archbishop Oscar Arnulfo Romero:

These homilies will be the voice of the people. They will be the voice of those who do not have a voice. Without a doubt my words will be poorly received by those who have too much of a voice. But this poor voice will resound in those who have the truth and love the truth of our dear people.[23]

And finally, Pope John Paul II, says:

For the Church, evangelizing means bringing the good news into all the strata of humanity, and through its influence, transforming humanity from within and making it new.[24]

Whether they are called Cursillos de Capacitación Social or by any other name, dynamic and democratic base communities have formed throughout Central America. Recently citizens of the United States have followed the Central American example. While less visibly religious than their Central America counterparts, thousands of new solidarity communities share the spirituality and faith as they stand up to Goliath in the person of David.

I have chosen to call the members of these communities "guerrillas of peace" because that is what the Indians of Quiche in Guatemala chose to call our unarmed teams of university students, high school students, Indian organizers, priests, sisters and brothers.

Were it not for the great peace movement resisting the Indochina war, there would have been a nuclear holocaust—as Nixon admits in his memoirs. The women of Greenham Common are guerrillas of peace, the Greens of Germany are guerrillas of peace. The Holy Week Peace Marchers of Europe are guerrillas of peace. Internationally, such guerrillas of peace are identifying new and powerful instruments of change. These new instruments are humane and democratic. No one is looking for less democracy. What are some of these instruments? Personal investigative fact-finding, which includes going directly to the site of conflict; demythologizing current misconceptions; dialogical study groups, seminars, and conferences; the production of documentary and dramatic films, not simply to inform and make value judgements, but to raise consciousness; sermons in churches which clearly ask people to decide which side they are on; radio and television presentations which do not begin with the presumption of the divine inspiration of U.S. foreign policy; invitations to foreign visitors to come to the United States and to make their points personally; publication of articles in mass media and scholarly journals; medical and legal aid programs; lobbying on issues and candidates. Instruments used should have some proportionality to the injustice that is to be corrected.

Cultural expression is of the essence. There is no authentic movement without a mystique. The New Song of Latin America is an excellent example. New Wave and Rock are not without consciousness. Poetry, drama, and art of all kinds are instructive avenues of expression. Demonstrations and rallies require culture and humor.

Beyond these activities of electoral and mass mobilization politics are the powerful tools of the strike and the boycott. Perhaps the greatest instrument of non-violent change is the general strike. Nothing could be more democratic. The general strike is simply the paralysis of society until such time as the cry for justice is heard and acted upon.

These powerful tools of change have been used around the world—by Ghandi, Martin Luther King, and Bishop Desmond Tutu. They are being used today in the diabolical repression of Guatemala, and in that facade of democracy which covers the dictatorship called El Salvador.

The group of prominent citizens founded by Father Miguel d'Escoto and called "the twelve" had the audacity to return to Managua publicly while Somoza was still in power. Somoza's henchmen must have known that d'Escoto was already representing the FSLN (Sandinista National Liberation Front) internationally. The dictatorship was literally afraid to attack the Foreign Minister of the guerrillas as he and his eleven companions were received by masses of cheering citizens.

In spite of all the killings, threats and torture, Guatemalan and Salvadoran citizens are still conducting street demonstrations. What an example to the peace movement. What if all of these great and powerful non-violent instruments of change fail? Ask the base communities of Chalatenango in El Salvador. What did they do? Like peasants all over the world, they didn't look lightly upon taking up arms. In the spirit of the base community, they gathered together in the name of God to pray and meditate on the problem. "Do we have the right to let someone kill us?" was the first question. And after dialogue the group concluded they did have the right to let someone kill them. After all Jesus must have allowed himself to be killed. Next question: "Do we have the right to allow someone to kill our parents, children, or our old grandmother?" This is a different situation. To allow such a thing would mean complicity with violence. Hence, after much discussion, the group concluded they were not free, they did not have the luxury of letting someone kill their own.

This kind of base community discussion is not a parlor game...not a trivial pursuit. It is a life and death communication. It may be the role of helicopters in their country and what they are to do about those helicopters. The conclusion is that they cannot be responsible for the ignorance or diabolical possession of those who sent the helicopters in to kill their children. But the helicopters must go. The readers will perhaps remember early in the Salvadoran conflict that the entire fleet of U.S. helicopters was destroyed in El Salvador in a striking rebel attack.

Yes, guerrillas of peace prefer the instruments of non-violent change. It is always a tragedy when hellish circumstances force lovers of peace and justice to use the old fashioned weapons of change.

—1—
Democratic Pedagogy:
The Birth of Liberation Theology

Baptism of Water Is Not A Necessity

In Central America, liberation theology is learned by the ancient method: walk around, live, and thus learn as we dialog, think and suffer.[1] Personally speaking, I recall clearly concluding while in the village of Aguacatan, that I would rather vaccinate than baptize a child. In spite of the worst of imperial theology, and the view that baptism of water was some sort of absolute necessity, lest one be condemned to Limbo, we knew, perhaps instinctively, that baptism by water was not a necessity. We knew that all these children and adults of Aguacatan were part of the family of God, and that while some ritual might be in order to express their membership in that family, it was a question of celebrating membership, not mandating it.[2]

The tool selected for reaching the university community in Guatemala was the Cursillo de Capacitación Social. The Guatemalan program came from Caracas, Venezuela and was initially designed by Father Manuel Aguirre S.J. The Cursillo de Capacitación program was designed to introduce university students to social questions via a Roman Catholic analysis.[3] While not an apologia for the Christian Democratic Party, the Cursillo de Capacitación Social was most compatible with Christian Democratic ideology. As we noted earlier, in the period from 1962 through 1967 the program was a polemic response to marxian analysis and the materials from Caracas were rigidly anti-marxist.

However, the students at the University of San Carlos were already practicing democracy within their organization. The student center was called the Crater or *Centro de Capacitación Social* and was originally part of the ecclesiastic structure of the church in Guatemala.[4] But the Crater was a base community in fact. The students would go over all the materials to be used in the cursillo, and translate the material into a mode that was understandable and applicable in Guatemala. A typical student comment: "There are two kinds of professors at this university: the marxists and those who simply don't give a damn." Such comments arose because of the personal admiration of the students for those who were attempting to build community in Guatemala using marxist analysis. And further, it was precisely these professors who were kidnapped and killed with shocking regularity.

The students did not doubt the sincerity of the Christian Democrats, especially those who frequented the center and assisted in the cursillo. In liberal fashion, however, the Christian Democrats generally supported all the objectives of justice and peace, but were not inclined to see the fundamental contradictions in the economic structures of Central America. There were Christian Democratic programs, called Pobladores, designed to help organize the poor in the miserable *barranca* slums of Guatemala City. These hellish mazes of tin, cardboard, excrement, children, bloated bellies, worms, sickness, and death were and still are home to hundreds of thousands of working people. While they acknowledged the concern of the Christian Democrats for these problems, the students of the Crater doubted that the Christian Democratic programs would ever transform the conditions which made these slums an unceasing reality in Central American life.[5]

Democracy was the central dynamic of the Crater, both as a Roman Catholic student center and as a birthplace of liberation theology. This democratic practice was visible in a constant flow of input from the base. For example, the students highlighted the class differences between religious personnel and the average Guatemalan worker or peasant. The students emphasized that they had never seen a hungry church person.

The elements of organized religion, which could be properly categorized as an opiate of the people, were a frequent subject of discussion: the poor were told to be patient as their children suffer malnutrition; while the rich could literally buy their sacraments. Even middle class Guatemalans were accustomed to ordering a special mass in the local parishes and paying a sum worth more than a month's salary for the average working person. It was not unusual for the donor to tell the churchman what he or she would like to hear in the sermon. Often they would request a mass in Latin instead of in Spanish, and they would get what they bought.

Pastors would express their disdain for this kind of retail religiosity, even as they recognized that if they did not accept masses and other sacraments on this basis, they would not be able to maintain their parishes. The practice of simony was categorized as a form of ecclesiastical prostitution by progressive clergy.[6] Many felt it was better for them to earn their own keep by working with their hands as St. Paul did.

The theology of empire vested so much authority in the local bishop that many parishoners would spend much time speculating about improvements that would occur when the incumbent died. The practice of democracy in the local base communities, on the other hand, went on regardless of the viewpoint of the local bishop. Here there is no waiting for the bishop to die; there is simply acting and living as Christians.

The practice of democracy in the base communities will probably have greater implications for Christianity than did the Reformation of some five hundred years ago.[7] Base communities show little interest in defining the things of God in Heaven. The near-unanimous interest of people in base communities is their role in doing the will of God on earth. The arrogance and irreverence of defining God contradicts a community of love.

What was actually happening in Guatemala in the mid-60s—set against the backdrop of Vatican II—was the formation of a revolutionary Christianity, established through a relationship between the Christian faith and revolutionary thought as a result of practice and theoretical reflection. The dualisms of spirit/matter, body/soul, earth/heaven, religion/politics, salvation/revolution, and all of the other essentialist dualisms which block the conscience and impede the participation of Christians in the revolutionary process were erased. The objective was obviously the humanization of society.[8]

To The Mountains

A rock has a value as a creature of God. A stalk of corn has a value as a creature of God. A mule has a value as a creature of God. But the human person is the highest creature in the known world, and has a right to live better than the animals. (From Cursillo Curriculum)

The central question for the Guatemalan University students belonging to the Crater was how could their eight-day course be organized for Indians in the mountains? After much discussion, attention was focused on the method of Paulo Freire. Some of us had studied with him directly, and others were influenced by his book, *The Pedagogy of the Oppressed*, which first appeared in Portuguese, later to be translated into Spanish and English. Freire's method was the practice of democracy in education. His methodology fit perfectly with the exercise of democracy within the student center.

Because the university vacation period occurred in the months of November and December, students suggested that we spend a full six weeks in the mountain areas of Huehuetenango and Quiche. To our surprise, at the student center, over ninety students volunteered to serve in thirty villages in these two Indian departments.[9]

The departments of Quiche and Huehuetenango were selected. Instead of the eight-day program, a period of five days was structured for the Indian cursillos.

The availability of university students to work in the Indian areas depended on the schedule of the school year. In order to allow for more cursillos the ongoing program was structured around weekend courses. A typical weekend program in the Indian areas would include the most essential talks emphasizing the dignity of the human person, the common good, responsibility, the right to organize, and an introductory look at how to organize.[10] The first cursillos were for Spanish-speaking Indians. Hence, the majority of the recipients were male migratory workers who had some contact with urban centers.[11] The scene of the Indian cursillo was a local parish. Pastors would announce the event to their parishoners, and generally parishioners would attend out of respect for their priests.

Many of the villages selected were so isolated that there was no access other than small footpaths. We were pleased to realize on many occasions that after a few days in one of these isolated villages, visitors would come from other villages to request our presence with them as well.

We had been concerned that the burden of three educators in a village might be too much for the Indian people. We simply asked that the three teachers in each village be given food and a place to sleep. I do not know of a single instance where the students were not accepted. Sharing is a way of life in the Indian community.[12]

I was embarrassed by the reverence the Indians showed toward me when they discovered I was a priest. On some occasions they insisted I ride a horse when everyone else was walking. But the students had ways of dealing with any elitism I might exhibit. On one occasion we were organizing in the community of La Libertad in Huehuetenango. A messenger came down from the mountain village of Aguacate asking for a priest to give the last sacraments to a dying elder. I went up to Aguacate on a mule with two guides. There was no road and often the trail was too steep for a mule. Upon arrival I was directed to the bedside of the old gentleman. The entire community was involved in making his confession for him: "He was good to his children," "He was faithful to his wife," "He would get angry some times," "He drank too much," and on and on from various and unsolicited relatives and friends. The old gentleman did not say much and would wince occasionally at some delicate comment. Trying to maintain a somber expression, I gave absolution and bid the small community goodbye after some tortillas and fresh milk. The trip to Libertad was without incident. But as I came to the church grounds, I was ambushed. Some five students attacked with firecrackers. The mule lost his patience and I was in the dust. I have always been struck by the ability of Central Americans to joke and even to light firecrackers in the midst of the struggle. The message has never been forgotten. We may be in danger but we will not reject song, poetry, and laughter.

A five-day preparatory session was scheduled at the Christian Brothers School in Huehuetenango. We continued to adapt the methodology of Paulo Freire to the Guatemalan Indian. Where Freire called for photographic slides representing aspects of local life, we settled for posters.[13] Otherwise, we were prepared much as he advised. Thus the six-week program included Freire's process of Alfabetizacion and Conscientización: social and political awareness training, together with literacy training.

The Freirian method is built around group dialogs, designed to stimulate thinking about everyday realities, and thereby raise consciousness. The following is a typical dialog to illustrate the dignity of the human person:

> Q: "Do you have any sick horses on this finca?"
> A: "Yes. We have some sick horses."
> Q: "What happens to a sick horse?"
> A: "A horse doctor takes care of the horse."
> Q: "Have you had any sick children on this trip to pick cotton?"
> A: "Yes. Two of our children died on this trip."
> Q: "Was there a doctor for the sick children?"
> A: "No."
> Q: "Then your child is of less value than a horse?"
> A: "Of course not."[14]

Examples of the importance of unity were given: first, breaking individual sticks easily and then placing many sticks together to show how difficult it was to break a bundle of sticks. The ladino (of mixed Spanish and Indian descent) teachers would express respect for things which the Indians traditionally did collectively. When they build houses, everyone helps. When times are bad, everyone shares. To build on the community culture of the Indian people, cursillo teachers would make comparisons to the nature of the Liga Campesina, or Peasant League. The Peasant League gives peasants power in the same way that many sticks held together have power; in the same way sharing gives power.

Some of the Indian communities were familiar with the dangers of labor organization in Guatemala. Ever since the United States intervention of 1954, (ably described by Stephen Schlesinger and Stephen Kinzer in *Bitter Fruit*, by Jim Handy in *Gift of the Devil*, and by Richard Immerman in *The CIA in Guatemala*) there has been a saying in the countryside: "The best place to visit organizers of rural labor is in the cemeteries."

An understanding of the collective nature of sin was clearly developing among both the urban students and the rural Indians. A synonymous relationship of sin, injustice, and oppression emerged: It was sinful for children to die of malnutrition and curable diseases. It was sinful to have no access to land when so much was available. It was sinful not to be able to read, to write, to communicate with our brothers and sisters in the one human family. This sort of verbalization of the collective nature of sin was a landmark in Indian consciousness-raising.[15] Related to this was consciousness-raising around the reality of institutionalized violence.

Theology of empire stressed personal sin and personal guilt at the expense of understanding or even perceiving institutional sin. Perhaps least acknowledged were the sins of the Church itself: its class structure; its poor distribution of its resources; its distribution of material goods to the clergy rather than to all of the community; its heretical demands on the faithful, which include constantly changing its moral messages though each new one is spoken with an irrevocable certitude, thus showing a lack of respect for the people themselves.[16]

Speaking of the perfection of the teaching authority of the Church throughout the 20th century, without speaking of the constant sins, errors, and omissions of the institutional body, would be similar to speaking of the foreign policy of the United States in the same period as equally perfect. In both cases, had there been an effectively communicative relationship with the people, we would have expected a higher level of performance. But the greatest evil in both the case of Church and State is the triumphalism and presumed moral perfectionism of the institution. At play is a vestige of the Divine Right of Kings combined with a warped sense of ideological infallibility.

La Mano Blanca: Terrorism as State Policy

It was in the department of Huehuetenango that the Indians first named the teams of the Cursillo de Capacitación Social "guerrillas of peace." The Indians knew the university students from the Crater were unarmed, but they also understood the goals and objectives of the group to be revolutionary and so the name arose.[17] For the rightist death squads, there was to be no distinction between armed struggle and non-violent struggle.

By 1967, the cursillos had extended to the Department of Zacapa. In contrast to the Indian highlands of the northwest of Guatemala, this area was Ladino in character. A five-day cursillo was carried out in the town of Gualan, but the program was short-lived. The student chairman in the area received a letter from La Mano Blanca (the

White Hand), noting that he had been selected by the organization to be killed.[18]

Receiving word of this occurrence at my office in Guatemala City, I decided to make a trip to the Gulan area to see if it were possible to meet the director of La Mano Blanca. With the help of the local church, I was indeed able to get a hearing with Mariano Sanchez, head of La Mano Blanca. Heavily armed aides brought me to the modest home of the leader of the clandestine death squads.

"Do you know of the meetings we have had at the church?" I asked. "Yes," he answered. "We have been talking about social progress," I asserted. Mariano Sanchez replied, "I am for progress." Behind the death squad leader was a picture of Castillo Armas. The picture had become the symbol of the National Movement of Liberation or MLN, which was the party of Castillo Armas, the beneficiary of the 1954 U.S. intervention in Guatemala. The land reform which United Fruit Company had so dreaded was abruptly cut short. The reforms which democratically elected President Jacobo Arbenz championed were undone. Arbenz and electoral democracy were undone. Guatemala now had Armas, and Sanchez and the death squads too. Washington was happy at the success of its intervention.[19]

I asked Sanchez if he knew the student who had received the death squad threat. At first he denied knowing the student, but after a bit more discussion, he stated matter-of-factly, "He is a communist." I asked him why he would make that statement and he finally said, "We know him. His brother went to Havana. We know that type." After lengthy discussion, the aide at Mariano's right hand said, "I know he's a communist because I heard him say he would give his life for the poor."

Personally, this meeting was for me a moment of consciousness-raising, not unlike those moments many others touched by the Crater had likely experienced—a gut-level unequivocal realization that the conflict in Guatemala was actually a war between the rich and the poor, and that the poor and those involved with the work of the poor were universally categorized as communists. Later, crossing the Motagua River by canoe, after the meeting with Mariano Sanchez, I was convinced that I was alive only because I was a United States citizen and a priest. In coming years, neither of those categories would have helped.

Upon return to the Crater in Guatemala City, I shared my conviction with the students that self-defense would be necessary should they return to the area of Gualan. A collective decision followed to continue work in the Indian areas of Quiche and Huehuetenango and to leave the Department of Zacapa for the time being. Actually, by 1967, the Zacapa area had an eight-year history of war which began November 13, 1960, and continued uninterrupted. We were of the opinion that the Mano Blanca and the military would make a distinction between our unarmed projects and guerrilla warfare. They did not.[20]

As of the summer of 1966, we were able to generalize from experience that the members of La Mano Blanca carried a card confirming membership as a Comisionado Militar. That is to say that each and every member of this allegedly secret death squad organization was actually under the direction of the armed forces of Guatemala. In turn, of course, the armed forces of Guatemala were directly connected to the CIA through CONDECA (The Central American Defense Council). I was beginning to leave my political adolescence behind. The terrorists in Guatemala were representatives of the State. The State was a dutiful servant of the U.S. Executive Branch of government. From the reality of Guatemala I began to understand the rape of Indochina. The worst crimes weren't extremist acts carried out by fanatics. Rather, these crimes and their perpetrators were all part of policy. It was policy, U.S. policy, that was the root of our problems. And it was no aberration.

Typical Schedule of a Guatemalan
Cursillo De Capacitación

6:00 Rising. (These were co-ed programs. There were male and female dormitories.)

6:05 Calisthenics. (Generally under the direction of a Comandante; an experienced student leader.)

6:30 Wash, Dress.

7:00 Meditation. (Generally taken from the New Testament and directed by a priest, sister, or student.)

7:30 Breakfast (All take turns in serving, cooking, and cleaning up.)

8:30 Inquiry. (e.g. urban..."Are we bourgeois?" rural... "Do horses live better than campesinos?")

9:00 First Class. (What is the Guatemalan reality?)

10:00 Second Class.

11:00 Third Class.

12:00 Group Discussions.

12:30 Sports. (Co-ed.)

1:00 Lunch.

2:30 Inquiry. ("Are demonstrations effective? Is the faith compatible with revolution?")

3:00 Fourth Class.

4:00 Fifth Class.

5:00 Extemporaneous talks required of participants. Situational titles given to each student. For example, "You are the leader of a demonstration. The army opens fire. What instructions do you give your demonstators?"

6:30 Mass. (A revolutionary celebration including guitars, folk hymns and an orientation to liberation. The sermon is a dialogue with all participants.)

7:10 Dinner.

8:00 Entertainment. (All participate in songs, dances, games, jokes.)

9:00 Debate. (e.g. "Is the armed struggle a necessity?")

10:00 Review of the Day and Self Criticism. (This includes general criticisms of the program, personal confrontations with individuals who have shown a lack of discipline, and acknowledgement of errors by those who feel they have not been fully participant.)

10:30 Retire.

Sample topics covered in classes:

The Social Problem; The Family; Liberalism; Communism; Capitalism; The Social Doctrine of the Church; The Formation of a Christian Social Sense; Love; Marxism; Socialism; Agrarian Reform; Revolution; Why Must We Change the Structures of Society?; The Dignity of the Human Person; A Christian Philosophy of Life; Social and Political Statistics on Guatemala; El Salvador; Nicaragua; Honduras; Costa Rica; Panama; The Common Good; Responsibility; Action.

After completing the eight day urban program, students were invited to become part of the on-going teams for bringing the Cursillos to the indian area. A variety of programs were designed: Days of action where it was only possible to meet for one day; five day programs for the Indian areas in the mountains; brief meetings on the meaning of peasant organization and the formation of peasant unions. The most vulnerable people were the Indian labor leaders. They could generally speak three or four Indian languages and were held in great reverence by all.

—2—
The Emerging Revolutionary
Personality and Ethic

"...wise as serpents and simple as doves..."
Matthew 10; 16

Some observers of our methods asked why we did not leave the Indians to their "purity" and "isolation," but it was our conviction that no one was leaving the Indians alone. Intrusions were being made on their land; mineral and petroleum searches were continuous, and they were being treated in a racist manner. Any presumption that the Indian would be left alone was unrealistic.

Our "dialogical pedagogy" demanded that we be constantly learning from the Indian, and we did. Dialog demands mutual love. Students were urged to imbibe of the Indians' culture and to respond to the Indians' hopes, anxieties, and desires.

Only with hindsight is it possible to see that what was taking place in Quiche and Huehuetenango in 1967 was an integration of urban Ladino university students, Indian campesinos, and, to the surprise of cursillo organizers, guerrillas from isolated *focos* (bases). The resulting dialogical communication contributed to the formation of a collective revolutionary personality in Guatemala.

As a participant in the Guatemalan struggle during the mid-60s, I was of the opinion that Indian people would only see liberation in terms of ethnicity. I did not believe Indians could integrate their primarily ethnic goals and objectives with the broader, sometimes threatening, aims of urban Ladino people. Time has proven that while there are major obstacles to Indian-Ladino cooperation, nonetheless I was overly pessimistic about the possibilities.

In the case of Nicaragua, Miskito, Sumu, and Rama Indians who were not participants in the struggle against Somoza now embody a strong counter-revolutionary potential. To the uninformed, the "Spaniards" from Managua had won the revolution. Yet, Indians of the same ethnic backgrounds who joined the Sandinista cause developed a collective revolutionary personality. The struggle itself was their school. The critical difference is participation.

Sandinista leaders identify many errors in their early work with the Indians of the Atlantic Coast. Most Sandinistas were ignorant of Indian life and thought only in terms of class struggle. But folk communities are not reached simply on the basis of class struggle. Much of the problem is anthropological.

33

I found many analogies between our practices in the institutional Church and the practices of the Indian folk communities. Both wore distinctive garb. The garb was so important in Guatemala that those who changed their garb were legally no longer considered Indians. Indeed, some Indians dropped their native dress in an attempt to escape racist repression. Blood was not the only determinant of community membership. Life style played an important role. Realizing this even helped me understand why religious garb meant so much to conservative elements in the ecclesiastical hierarchy. Folk life is conservative. Elders in religious life and in isolated Indian villages have great authority and are treated with reverence. New ideas are not generally welcome. Someone bringing a wheelbarrow into a folk community might be reminded that women carry burdens on their heads and men carry burdens on their back.

Custom means a great deal in such lifestyles. Folk communities are comfortable. Identity is clear. People know who they are. As a result, acculturation is rare in Guatemala. Outsiders are met with caution. They can threaten the very existence of a folk community. A road may sound useful but it may also be the avenue by which traditional lands disappear. There is wisdom in folk cultures whether they are villages in northwest Guatemala or religious orders in industrialized countries. But the wisdom can also be compromised by ignorance. And, in any event, this wisdom is not enough to match the modern extermination techniques of Alvarado, Mejia Victores, or other Guatemalan dictators.

Folk cultures have been survival-oriented; they have not been international in orientation. It is this international aspect that awaits development. Can the new person be developed who identifies as strongly with the human race as with the folk village, even as he or she keeps local ethnic wisdom alive? The revolutionary personality believes this is possible. It is possible to identify with all children as with one's own children. It is possible to identify with all sick people as with one's family. It is possible to identify with people of one's own culture according to one's own ethnic customs, and with everybody else according to the norms of respect and fellowship as well. The familial extension of one's concern and care is indicative of an expansion of consciousness, or what Tielhard de Chardin calls a more cranial society.

Yet, certainly the history of revolutionary change is not without dissension in the ranks:

> And the whole community of the Sons of Israel began to complain against Moses and Aaron in the wilderness and said to them, "Why did we not die at Yahweh's hand in the land of Eqypt, when we were able to sit down to pans of meat and could eat bread to our hearts content? As it is, you

have brought us to this wilderness to starve this whole company to death!" (Exodus 16; 2-4)

Conscious Indians throughout Guatemala know their liberation requires not simply the liberation of their linguistic or cultural background. Ethnic identity is certainly necessary for the formation of an integral personality. But political reality must also go beyond ethnic identity. To be catholic, a polity must have equal consideration for all within its geographical borders.[1]

It would be unrealistic and even boring to imagine a homogenized socialist culture as a basis for international solidarity. The key is "autonomy within solidarity." Indigenous people can and should enjoy their life-styles as they simultaneously maintain and also transcend their folk cultures, maintain ethnic autonomy and also enter into the political economy of the present day.

The revolutionary personality is unashamedly humanistic. In the highlands of Guatemala communion between atheistic humanists and theistic humanists was realized. This humanistic base is the foundation of what can be called liberation theology.[2] It is from this base that the Christian can understand the message of Jesus and his incarnation. It is from this base that the atheist or non-theist can communicate with the believing population. Human need is the basis of an authentic economy. Human need is the correct motive for production. Human need is the reason for a political order. It was precisely this humanism that led to the Christian marxist dialog and praxis in Central America.

Some religious fundamentalists reject such humanism as a heresy. They believe it is possible to begin with the premise that one *has* the truth. The disastrous effects of such an absolutist position is obvious in the history of the Roman Inquisition, contemporary Iran and contemporary Israel.

The "Electronic Church" in the United States is rampant with attacks on humanism as a basis for religious understanding. Ranting and raving against humanism is unrealistic and only substitutes sentimentality for love. It seems safe to say, "Those who attempt to define God are always wrong. Those who attempt to love their brothers and sisters of the human race are often right." Primitive Christian or liberation theological analysis cleansed of its imperial trappings acknowledges that this love of fellow person is at once love of God. The entire twenty-fifth chapter of Saint Matthew's Gospel emphasizes this point.[3]

Once the base of humanism is established, a society which interjects money between its people and their education can only be categorized as outdated. Once a human base is accepted, a society which allows money to interfere with universal health care can only be categorized as outdated. Profit for the few simply does not conform to fundamental human standards. What is currently called liberation theology has been developed, at least in part, by living with the poor. Abstract dualisms begin to suffer as a result of concrete reflections. The following is a personal diary entry made in the highlands of Huehuetenango, October 12, 1966: "Many matters require my attention and it seems to me that by writing, I may be able to firm up attitudes of my spiritual life. I even hesitate to use the world 'spiritual' because every event, every breath is involved. Perhaps I had simply better say, 'life'."

I was not inclined to write such phrases from my prior position as a regional superior in the United States. I wrote on the same day: "Two camps are obvious among the priests, sisters and religious people in this poor country: those who don't even see the problem, and who might believe that military power can eliminate the forces of revolution, and those who sympathize with the revolution to the extent they might even join it. True, there are many idealists within the FAR, but it is not the place of the religious to join in with this ideology." I could not help but think of the Fifth Chapter of the First Book of Macabees: "On that day, some priests fell in battle; trying to do something heroic, they had gone out unadvisedly to fight."[4]

On October 18, 1966, from the same primitve mountain location, I wrote: "A revolution is taking place throughout the world, and it would be a pleasure to be part of it. To help give direction to the church and churchmen who are groping and wondering just what their role will be.... And now, to be here in Guatemala; a privilege and honor to serve the Lord 'to the ends of the earth,' I do not intend to become accustomed to the poverty and destitution of these poor people. I do not intend to become accustomed to their sickness, ignorance, to the constant injustices they receive. I do intend to do whatever I can to change these evils. God help me to be wise as a serpent and simple as a dove."[5]

These personal reflections demonstrate the influence of the Guatemalan people and the situation on my personal theological development. It was the combination of forces acting on me, the spirit of the people's resistance, that was special.

One of the characteristics of contemporary liberation theology is the importance of making history. History is not something to watch as a spectator but to participate in. There is no distinction between sacred history and secular history. The history of the human race is integral. There are many possible futures and these possibilities depend on the level of consciousness of individuals and on their collective efforts. We are responsible for our fates.[6]

Communion with the Indians of Aguacatan resulted in a sense of personal liberation and sublime purpose. I wrote on October 15, 1966, in the Cuchimantanes Mountains: "Indians, naturales, Indigines, people of mystery, people of spirit, intuitive people. Aguacatan, how many eons of people have lived within your sacred boundaries? People of the Jaguar, dominated by the Mayan priests; people of Zaculeo, dominated by the Conquistadores, people of Maiz, dominated by Ladino; poor in spirit, meek and humble of heart, hungry people who do not know how to beg. Sick people looking for a cure but not ready to acknowledge sickness until at death's door. Farmers of garlic, lovers of children, experts at prayer. You do not read, you do not write, but you understand. Yes, you understand better than I and you see. You see through everyone; you see through me. You read thoughts, you ask for nothing and you laugh. You laugh together, you laugh with each other and you laugh at the world. The rest of the world does not know your many vowels. Your language belongs to you alone. No one understands it, no one speaks it but you, Aguacateco!

"And what secrets you have, no one can share them. No one can penetrate them. Your riches; you noble and dignified, old and young; you suffer yourselves to be packed into trucks, to be hustled to the strange sea-level lands to pick for a pittance, to pick coffee and receive malaria, to pick bananas and receive a scorpion!

"I have an idea about you, Indian, you will sit and judge the world. You will be its judgement.

"You pay three cents tax to sit in the marketplace and sell chocolate and you have earned five cents in six hours. You pay your tax and you receive your receipt, but you are hungry, Aguacateco; can you never get angry? Will you ever learn resentment? Your child cannot eat the tax receipt. Your mother's breast is dry and you will die, nino. You will die and never be able to carry wood as your daddy does. He can carry 100 pounds and he does not wear shoes, they are so expensive. But he will earn $100 in a year, $100 in pennies. But this year, this wet year, he will have to buy corn, pennies for so little corn.

"He has title to half an acre. It is all his and he is proud of his land. But thirty acres would be what he needs. Complain? You do no not know the word. Your patience appalls me! Your silence stuns me. Your contemplation embarrasses me.

"Did you take a vow of poverty? Perhaps you are not telling. Did you make a pact with the Lord to be the monastery of the world?

"I would have you awake to the hatred around you. I would have you crush the injustice that you live and breathe. I would have you rise up as a person and refuse to serve in slavery. But you are so much better than I that you love your enemies and do good to those who hate you.

"Aguacatan, teach me one of your thousand secrets! Teach me one of your sacred ways."

Once a process of personal liberation begins, an exterior expression seems necessary. To even consider attempting to hear the confessions of thousands of Indians individually was truly oppressive.

Often they would speak their own language, a language I did not understand. Sometimes they would speak in Spanish, but this was always a recitation of routine, personal faults. As a result of dialogs with cursillo members, a collective liturgical celebration of confession or the sacrament of penance was begun. This joyful experience included the singing of hymns; reflections on sins, both personal and, especially, collective and institutional; resolve to make the changes necessary in self and institution; and one final absolution for whatever number of people was present.

Hence, within fifteen or twenty minutes, we could accomplish what would have taken days were it done on an individual basis. But even more important was the fact of the meaningful nature of the celebration and its actual historical relationship to ecclesiastical tradition. We could not help but call to mind the provision in the Code of Canon law for giving absolution to a company of troops ready to go into battle. We considered the Indians, the members of Cursillo de Capacitación Social, and the members of the FAR to all be in serious physical danger. This gave us *a fortiori* rationale for the practice.

Legalisms which were allowed to stifle the life of organized religion in its middle class settings in the United States and Europe have been replaced in much of the Third World with a virtue. That virtue is called *epikeia*. It is actually a dispositon of the person which includes a noble inclination of the heart. It is deciding to always make the juridical serve justice,[7] to keep the law in service of conscience and, whenever required, to give unconditional priority to the eternal law of nature written in a person's heart. The decision: virtue will reign over every positive text of the law. Neither a legalistic society nor a legalistic institutional church cares to speak much about the virtue of *epikeia,* whereby church people can involve themselves in the risks of evolving global events and abandon the paternalistic forms of colonizing missionary activity in order to become a catholic world body, a home for people of all cultures.

One of the contributions of the Central American people, especially the Indian people, to the formation of liberation theology, is the belief in a common good. In practice, for most people the message is little more than rhetorical. But the belief in and practice of the common good is *fundamental* in the formation of the revolutionary personality. The adversarial mind of individualism is apt to say, "Your common good is not my common good." What becomes obvious, however, from the perspective of poverty, is the almost unanimous agreement on matters relating to common good. There is little argument about the need for warm clothing among the people of the highlands. There is a craving to become literate. There is a respect for hygiene, public health measures, parental education, the study of nutrition, and the availability of food.

A diary entry of December 19, 1966: "It is clear we are in conflict with some of the folk religious practices.[8] It is interesting for us to be teaching reading, writing, tailoring, and arithmetic to those who are interested. This is done at the very time the Christmas posada processions are going by. Our group of lay Apostles are not in the "religious" demonstration, but rather in an educational process. And we think we have the mind of Christ. Such religious processions have gone on for centuries and seem truly marginal in their effectiveness; more important: education."

The Question of Violence

Discussions about violence, as discussions about religion, are generally rampant with hypocrisy. I do not recall ever hearing any religious objections to violence from church figures as I joined the United States Marines in the 1940s. On the contrary, there were constant expressions of pride on the part of Roman Catholic priests who served as chaplains and from local Catholic schools and parishes. The high percentage of Roman Catholics in the Marine Corps was considered to be a sign of the love of God and country maintained by Roman Catholics in the United States.

The political socialization of a people becomes obvious as we reflect on the fact that the nuclear bombing of Hiroshima and Nagasaki is not considered a practice of violence or terrorism. Generally, instead, the use of the word "terrorism" is reserved for small groups of people attempting to defend their interests in the midst of overwhelming opposition. In both imperial politics and imperial religion, contemporary Davids are referred to as terrorists and contemporary Goliaths as peace keepers.

An individual speaking on behalf of the right to self-defense of an oppressed people is tagged an advocate of violence. An individual speaking on behalf of increasing astronomical outlays on weapons of destruction that can only be used for intervention abroad or for armaggedon, is honored as a rationalist of peace. But the reality of Central America is not an exercise in debating. We cannot ask the question whether there will or won't be violence in Central America. Violence is as present there as disease, indeed, it is a social disease. Hence, it is not a matter of discussing the possibility of violence, but rather of identifying violence in its full reality. Many individuals who consider themselves nonviolent and religious are mistaken on both counts.

The success of the Cursillo de Capacitación Social in the departments of Huehuetenango and Quiche had reached such proportions by mid-1967 that the international press described the "guerrillas of peace" as an alternative to the violence of Central America. But

United States aid and the Guatemalan military sought a military solution: the clandestine death squads. Up to this point, the programs designed by the Centro de Capacitacion Social were public. In the later half of 1967, the situation was such that any continuation of the program would have to be done in a clandestine fashion.

In many places on this globe, a revolutionary personality is being formed in people who are simply becoming familiar with an authentic application of the New Testament.[9] It seems to me that the Christ theme is one of the basic currents of history. Truth may be expressed in art or in politics. Genuine minds, people of good will, listen, see and rejoice in the splendor of whatever truth is expressed. But as Albert Einstein said, "Great spirits have always encountered violent opposition from mediocre minds."

The mission of good news to the poor is obviously one of curing the sick, feeding the hungry, comforting the sorrowful; even bringing joy to a wedding where the celebrants ran out of wine. Jesus saw that they had more wine. But some picayune creatures who observed him simply wanted to catch him. For them, life's only goal was to assert their ego. Any action, miraculous or natural, by anyone not under their power was simply a threat. We read in Mark 3, 6:

> The pharisees went out and at once began to plot with the Herodians against him, discussing how to destroy him.

Early in Christ's ministry those whose only religion was their ego had plans to destroy him. And such is the case today. The goals of the people of Central America are simply health, education, and a human society. In the process of seeking these goals, they are being crucified. This is the Christ theme today. Everyone of goodwill knows that Washington's policy is simply the boot of empire on an innocent people. What is required of the U.S. is accepting the good news which is being brought to and arises from the poor. Our job is to get out of the way. Yet, Washington's program is one of invincible ignorance, including racism and greed. Let's take a look at a fundamental teaching of Jesus relating to the formation of the revolutionary personality. In Luke, 6, 27:

> But I say to those of you who are listening: Love your enemies, do good to those who hate you, bless those who curse you, pray for those who treat you badly. To the man who slaps you on one cheek, present the other cheek too; to the man who takes your cloak from you, do not refuse your tunic. Give to everyone who asks you, and do not ask for your property back from the man who robs you. Treat others as you would like them to treat you. If you love those who love you, what thanks can you expect? Even sinners lend to sinners to get back the same amount. Instead, love your

enemies and do good, and lend without any hope of return. You will have a great reward, and you will be sons of the Most High, for he himself is kind to the ungrateful and the wicked.

Be compassionate as your Father is compassionate. Do not judge, and you will not be judged yourselves; do not condemn and you will not be condemned yourselves; grant pardon, and you will be pardoned.

Give and there will be gifts for you: a full measure, pressed down, shaken together, and running over, will be poured into your lap; because the amount you measure out is the amount you will be given back.

I don't know of any group fulfilling these words more perfectly than the young people of Central America who are winning the struggle today. These are people who do good to those who hate them. I was stunned by the conduct of Tomas Borge, a leader of the Sandinista Revolution in Nicaragua. After years of struggle, he, the victor, confronted the man responsible for torturing him nearly to the point of death. "What revenge do I have for you?" said Borge. "I forgive you!"

Yes, the personality described here is a revolutionary personality. A revolutionary will tolerate a slap on the face. This is an excellent sign of self-control. Revolutionaries can be pushed, can be slapped, and they will control themselves. These are not street gangs, these are not bandits. These are revolutionaries. Yes, you can slap their face. But no; they were never instructed to allow someone to kill their children, to rape their wife, to torture and kill their husband, or to take their life. They are not stupid. And they are not unaware of the distinction between accepting an insult from some ignorant person as Christ is telling them to do, and allowing someone to take their life.

The revolutionary personality is a disciplined personality and a totally giving personality. While the youth of Central America distinguish themselves by their valiant lives and willing death; it is sad to see, in some cases, the youth in our own country selling themselves as objects. It's a shame to see sixteen-year-olds who look worn out, tired, sullen, sick, and violated.

If we are looking for an example of the Christ theme we can certainly find it by simply looking at some of the priests who have given their lives in Guatemala. It is not that the priests who have died have a greater value than the campesinos who have died. But the priests' deaths are more visible and give us a clear gauge of the level of morality of the governments supported by the United States with our tax money.

Our tax money went to kill Father Stan Rother in Guatemala. He was killed in Santiago Atitlan in the Department of Solola. Father Rother was from the diocese of Oklahoma and volunteered for work in

Guatemala. He had received death threats on numerous occasions and, in November of 1980, fears for his safety at the hands of members of the armed forces prompted Amnesty International to issue an urgent appeal on his behalf. His subsequent assassination is only one of a series of recent incidents reported to Amnesty International of harassment and murder directed against priests. On July 23, 1981, Amnesty International called upon the Guatemalan government to protect foreign and local religious personnel in view of this violence. There was no response.

Our tax money was responsible for the death of Father Marco Tulio Maruzzo who was machine-gunned in Quirigua on July 1, 1981, in northern Guatemala. This Franciscan missionary was killed after three gunmen stopped his car as he was returning to his parish. He had just taken catechists home after a prayer meeting. Father Maruzzo, 52, had been working in Guatemala since 1960. Shortly before his death he stated that he feared for his life. After his death his will revealed his foresight. It included the request that if he were killed, he should be buried in Guatemala as a testimony to government violence there.

On June 9, 1981, Father Luis Eduardo Pellecer, a Jesuit priest, "disappeared" in Guatemala City where he had been working with the residents of the Barrios Marginados (slum areas). Here we have a case of severe physical and psychological torture. After four months in prison at Carcel del Puerto de San Jose, the priest had appeared on government sponsored news to make a "confession." Duress was obvious.

In another instance of tax dollars doing their duty, a missionary of the Congregation of the Sacred Heart, Father Juan Alonso Fernandez, was abducted between San Miguel Uspantan and Cunen in northern Quiche on February 15, 1981. His abduction was witnessed by other passengers with whom he was traveling. The next day his body was found, shot to death, and bearing signs of torture. Father Juan Alonso Fernandez is only one of several Spanish missionaries of the Congregation of the Sacred Heart ordered to be killed in Quiche.

On January 11, 1981, the catechist of Santiago Atitlan in the Department of Solola was detained by four heavily armed men in a military jeep. Four other catechists were abducted the same day. People identified as having tried to aid the wives and children of the detained catechists have been threatened with death. Since their abduction there has been no news of their whereabouts.

On July 10, 1980, Father Faustino Villanueva, a Spanish priest also with the Sacred Heart Mission, was murdered by machine gun fire in Joyabaj, El Quiche.

On June 4, 1980, Father Jose Maria Gran Cirera was shot to death, along with his sacristan, Domingo Bats, as they were riding on horseback between Juil and Chajul. The Ministry of Defense alleged that they died in an armed confrontation between guerrillas and armed forces, but this was immediately denied by reliable sources in Guatemala who pointed to the great number of priests, nuns, and catechists placed under threat of death by government direction.

On May 12, 1980, Father Walter Voordeckers, an outspoken supporter of peasant rights, was brutally murdered near his church. He worked with the local population in setting up agricultural cooperatives in the department of Esquintla. He had been branded a "communist" and death threats were painted on the walls of his church. He made the error of helping the poor.

Father Conrado de la Cruz and his assistant, Herlindo Cifuentes, were kidnapped, along with forty-four other people on May 1, 1980. The bodies of many of the detained have been found. The priest is still missing.

I mention these priests—all abducted, tortured or killed in such a brief span, as others have been and continue to be now—not to give these few any more importance than any man or woman in Central America. I do so to show that the moral and ethical position taken by conscious clergy makes them a great threat to the existing order. None of these men would have died were they practicing theology of empire.

The revolutionary personality that attracts assassins' anger, even as it combats the conditions that breed assassination and poverty, is perhaps best expressed in poetry and song. Here is an example from El Salvador in a musical poem dedicated to the FMLN/FDR:

Si no vienes a dar
El corazon la vida
Si no vienes a dar
El corazon la vida
No te molestes en entrar

Porque en tu entrada
Comienza tu salida
Si tu vienes a buscar
Un lecho la ocasion mullida
No te molestes en entrar
Si tu vienes a buscar
Un lecho la ocasion mullida
No te molestes en entrar
Donde la flor mas bella
Es una herida

ESTRIBILLO:

Este es un lugar propicio
Tan solo para el sacrificio

Aqui tienes que ser el ultimo en comer
Aqui tienes que ser el ultimo en tener
Aqui tienes que ser el ultimo en dormir
Y el primero en morir

If you're not here to give
Your heart your life
If you're not here to give
Your heart your life
Don't bother coming in

Because in your coming in
Begins your going out
If you're here looking
For a good time lying around
Don't bother coming in
If you're here looking
For a good time lying around
Don't bother coming in
Where the most beautiful flower
Is a wound

CHORUS

This is a place favorable
Only for sacrifice
This is a place favorable
Only for sacrifice
Here you have to be the last one to eat
Here you have to be the last one to have
Here you have to be the last one to sleep
And the first one to die!

—3—
Becoming a Revolutionary Priest

On October 13, 1967, I placed the following entry in my diary. I reproduce it here as a firsthand account of some of the thinking that goes into the decision to become a revolutionary.

"I received an invitation from two student leaders of the group for which I am responsible. They asked, 'What will you do if we have to go underground?' I said, 'I will go with you.'

"And what does this imply? It implies carrying out the assignment I have been given. It implies not abandoning the flock; going where they go.

"Where does the concept of obedience come into this? I would have to act with autonomy. It is the function of authority to direct and coordinate the autonomy of individuals. But how can authority direct or coordinate in an area where authority has no competence? For example, only one working directly with students would be able to understand why they have a need to go underground. The decision would have to be made when the occasion arises. We cannot look to authority to answer questions that are not within its sphere. For example, a sister physician cannot ask her Mother Superior whether or not she should remove a gall bladder. Mother Superior does not know. The competent sister doctor must make the decision. Nor can I ask my superior whether I should go underground with my students. He does not have an understanding of the situation. Further, it is not the part of superiors to ask something above and beyond the call of duty, even in the military. Such decisions are made by men in the field of battle. And as a soldier may not know until after the battle whether he will gain a medal or a court martial, similarly, we cannot know whether, as the Apostle tells us, we are worthy of praise or blame.[1]

"We can only look at world history as something of a guide. We are members of a Church that was in its glory underground. The Christians were a threat to the most potent power structure of the day, the Roman Empire. Christian mystique was an attack on the very core of the political superstructure, which included the concept of emperor as a god. Not to acknowledge the emperor as a god was to strike at the roots of empire. Hence, Christians were martyred.

"The conversion of the Emperor Constantine marked the beginning of Imperial Christianity. Church people in the Western world have been associated with political power ever since. Catholic chaplains have served on both sides of armed conflicts in the Western world. By the 13th century, we see St. Thomas Aquinas speaking of the validity of religious orders founded for military purposes. Such orders existed.[2]

"Now if a group of intellectuals and students choose to be the voice of social justice and reform in a society whose very structures are evil, and if they request the presence of clergy to be their chaplains, should they not be heard? For practical reasons, it is not possible to ask the official spokesperson of the Church, that is, the Archbishop. He is neither competent intellectually nor politically able to give such a mandate. This request has to be made to an individual churchperson who is ready in conscience to accept. Here is a case for the use of the virtue of epikeia.

"In deciding whether or not to join the revolutionaries, the question must be asked, what effect will my action have on others? Latin Americans have a Catholic culture. The presence of a priest within a rebel group will undoubtedly encourage many who are yet unsure to join forces. The presence of a priest can give moderation, however, to the violence that is the unfortunate tool of revolution. It can also give qualities of forgiveness and not vengeance to the new order once established. It can also give acceptance of the Church to the new order, which may try to eliminate the Church were it not a part of the changeover. For example, Cuba has not eliminated the presence of the institutional Church. On the contrary, Cuba has official diplomatic ties with the Vatican, something that the United States does not maintain. [The Reagan administration has formalized diplomatic relations.] Cuba has eliminated Catholic schools; small damage. It has a certain anti-Church spirit, but it has a Church and zealous priests. We found priests in the mountains with Castro, and not only as chaplains but as fighting men. These men must have had a part in the toleration the Church has received in Cuba.[3]

"Nor should a priest in such a situation request laicization. He is doing something more than priestly. He is working directly in the action center of a people. He is relevant. We can thank the Spirit working in the hearts of revolutionaries that the priest is wanted in their struggle. His fear would be that they would tell him to stay home with the old women and children.

"These dedicated people have seen through the corruption of the institutional Church, and realize that even its archaic forms contain a message of salvation. In spite of the structures, they see the revolutionary spirit in Christ himself, the Man whose very existence was a challenge to the institutional Church of his time. This is the man who said,

> Do not suppose that I have come to bring peace to earth; it is not peace I have come to bring, but a sword. For I have come to set a man against his father, a daughter against her mother, a daughter-in-law against her mother-in-law. A man's enemies will be those of his own household. Anyone who prefers father or mother to me is not worthy of me. Anyone who prefers son or daughter to me is not worthy of me. Anyone who does not take his cross and follow in my footsteps is not worthy of me. Anyone who finds his life will lose it; anyone who loses his life for my sake will find it." (Matthew 10; 34-39.)[4]

"Yes, here is a decision that can only be made by the priest himself. Bureaucratic power structures cannot consider such a situation. Nor, in charity, could a superior be expected to give such a mandate. This mandate, unlike many others, must come from the community in question. That community is humbly asking. They know the consequences. They are not demanding.

"Am I qualified to say yes? Intellectually, I think so. I am one of two priests in the entire society with a graduate degree in Latin American studies. I have seen Latin America's problems in theory and in fact.

"Psychologically? Only God knows. I have never had any serious psychological problems. Physically? I have some physical problems, but a generally rugged composition. I have Marine training, and was cited in my training for outstanding performance in training maneuvers in very difficult terrain...

"Is it vanity? I love all comforts: Food, clothes, housing, etc. I do not relish the idea of living in the mountains like a hunted animal, without assurance of food, clothing, housing or life itself.

"But I am a North American. Yes, and I think this Witness is all the more needed by someone who bears the passport of a country now seen as the world's greatest assassin. U.S. citizens must object to what their country is doing. I would like a by-product of my presence to be a loud protest to U.S. involvement in Vietnam.

"Spiritually? I can only ask God for the power. It cannot be my own.

Foxes have holes and the birds of the air have nests, but the son of man has nowhere to lay his head." (Matthew 8; 20)[5]

Indeed, the hour is coming when anyone who kills you will think he is doing a holy duty for God. (John 16; 2)[6]

"Apparently, civil disobedience has always been in for followers of Christ. Indeed, it has been in scripturally and historically."

I reproduce here a document by Gaspar Garcia Lavinia published on February 2, 1978, that may shed further light on these points:

A Priest's Call To Arms—Gaspar Garcia Laviana

"During Christmas time, when we celebrate the birth of Jesus, Our Lord and Savior, who came into the world to announce the Kingdom of Justice, I want to speak to you as my brothers and sisters in Christ, and share with you my decision to enter the clandestine struggle as a soldier of the Lord and as a soldier of the National Liberation Front of Sandino.

"I came to Nicaragua from Spain, where I was born, to be a priest as a missionary of the Sacred Heart. I have served in this capacity for nine years. I threw myself into this apostolic work with great eagerness.

"Soon I discovered that the hunger and thirst for justice of the poor and oppressed people I served as priest demanded the counsel of action rather than the counsel of words.

"As an adopted Nicaraguan, I have seen the bleeding wounds of my people. I have seen the foul exploitation of farm workers crushed under the boot of landowners diligently protected by the National Guard, that instrument of injustice and repression. I have seen how a few enrich themselves obscenely in the shadow of the Somoza dictatorship. I have been a witness to the subjugation of lower-income youth in filthy carnal traffic, thrown into prostitution by the powerful. I have seen directly the vileness, deception and thievery of the Somoza family.

"They have been deaf to corruption and unmerciful repression, and they continue being deaf while my people are locked in each night in fear. My brothers and sisters suffer torture and prison for asking what is rightfully theirs: a country free and just in which robbery and murder disappear forever.

"Just as the finest young people of Nicaragua are at war against oppressive tyranny, I too have determined to join them and the lowest of the soldiers of the Sandino Front. I do this because it is a just war, a war which the Holy Gospels call good and in my conscience as a Christian it is good. I do this because it represents the struggle against conditions which are hateful to the Lord, Our God. I do this because the documents of Medellin, written by the Bishops of Latin America, taught,

"Revolutionary insurrection can be legitimate in the case of prolonged tyranny which gravely affects the fundamental rights of persons and endangers the common good of the country.

"I beg all my Nicaraguan brothers and sisters, for the love of Christ, that you support this struggle of the Sandino Front. The day of our people's redemption must not be delayed.

"To any sincere officials or soldiers of the National Guard who through fear or necessity serve the cause of Somoza, I say that now is the time to get on the side of justice, which is the side of Our Lord. To you businessmen who have not participated in the corruption, to you decent farmers, to the technicians and professionals who reject the chaos and despotism of Somoza, I say for everyone there is a place of struggle on the side of the Sandino Front to bring dignity to our country.

"To my brothers and sisters in the factories, in the shops, artisans, forgotten homeless people, those without jobs, those in the slums, the farm workers, the lumber workers, cane cutters and migrants—to all those who have been robbed of opportunity in this land—I say it is the hour to enter the ranks of the Sandino Front. Let us unite our hands and our arms. The sound of our rifles cry justice in the mountains, in the cities, and towns, and this sound is the sign of approaching redemption.

"The participation of everyone in this insurrection will result in new light and end the darkness of the Somoza dynasty.

"And to my brothers and sisters who are Sandinistas in the northern front of Carlos Fonseca Amador, and in the northeastern front of Benjamin Zeledon, and to the urban resistance sectors in our cities, I send my firm conviction that we are going to build a day of triumph through the sacrifice of our fallen heroes. They personify the will of our people to struggle. This struggle is with revolutionary dedication and sacrifice which we make together with the national leadership of the Sandinistas: Henry Ruiz (Brother Modesto), Daniel Ortega (Brother Enrique), and Tomas Borge (Brother Pablo), who is now in the Somoza slaughterhouse.

"The system of Somoza is sin. To liberate ourselves from oppression is to liberate ourselves from sin.

"With rifle in hand, full of faith and full of love for my Nicaraguan people, I will fight to the end for the coming of the reign of justice in our country, that reign of justice which the Messiah announced to us under the light of the Star of Bethlehem.

"A free country or death!"

Role Of The Revolutionary Priest

May our voices be the call to development which will make peace possible. May the Good Lord bless Pope Paul VI who made it clear that revolutionary uprisings are not out once all other means have failed.[7] May our work end the daily violence that surrounds us, the violence of destitution, ignorance and disease. May it tell the selfish that their party is over, and that they must now distribute the goods of the earth in justice.

In my diary, years ago, I commented about a trip to the United States, when I spoke to some thirteen priests and lay leaders about Guatemala. Without repeating their individual comments, I can surely state that the general response was positive. I spoke to these people about the invitation I had received from the Crater students to join their struggle. The only negative comment was made by an international lawyer. He asked if these people could be using the Church or churchpeople to their own advantages. I told him this was a very serious consideration, but perhaps the most significant characteristic of the rebels has been their authenticity. They have given up everything. Many have given up their lives for social justice. Their theoretical training may lead them to consider that any means are valid in bringing about the desired goal. And perhaps I should not remove this motive from all of them. But the group I have worked with has shown a dedicated and practical faith. They want the Church, they ask for the sacraments. Indeed, they may be the leaven, to give others whom I have not met, a deeper faith. I went on to make the following diary reflections:

"And what is the role of the priest-rebel? To be of service to his community, there will certainly be a sacramental ministry, and apart from this but joined with it, a ministry of the word. How much these people can identify with the words of Christ. They are taking up the sword and they know that they may perish by the sword. But did Jesus ever speak against taking up the sword? At the Last Supper, he asked them how many swords they had. Having a sword does not indicate that one does not have love. If it did, the Church would have had to give some witness against the sword. The Church has been associated with swords all through its history. It has spoken for peace, but never absolutely.

"Would a pacifist role be in order? To attempt to live as a 'holy man' in the midst of this strife? Perhaps this would apply personally. I would not have to bear arms. But a situation could be foreseen where, for the good of the community and its well being, arms might be in order even for its religious personnel. There are many cases of arms being issued to U.S. chaplains when they were with their men in hand-to-hand combat.

"The role of a guerrilla is a role in the temporal order. The laity must have autonomy in the temporal order. It is not the priests' role to mastermind their function in the social, economic or political fields. It is the priest's job to speak for forgiveness, peace, joy, love, service of others, faith, hope, charity, prayer, celebration of community, and the presence of Christ in the midst of those gathered in his name. Yes, this is priestly work in the midst of a painful situation. Innocent people will suffer. But will this not be the beginning of the end of the suffering of millions of innocents who now experience the misery of Latin America?

"Will this not be the way the United States (a country that I love deeply) will understand that a foreign policy of power politics and economic imperialism is simply out of date? Latin America will have a revolution that will be its own. It does not want domination from the Soviet Union, the United States or any other power. May the struggle of its most gifted citizens result in a government of the people, for the people and by the people.

"What about the limiting characteristic of association with an underground movement? As it is, I can talk to rich and poor, to the extreme right, to the left and to those with no opinion. But of what value? The attempt at dialogue at this point is seen by the people as almost hopeless. Generally, the rich want to continue in a feudal system that sees the poor as such by the will of God. They have not taken initiatives except to continue as they are. They consider mild programs like income tax, unions, and even coops, as forms of communism. Are they not like Dives: not willing to listen to anyone? They have the Word of God, but it seems they would not even listen to someone who rose from the dead.[8]

"About tactics? While this matter is ultimately up to the political community, it can be said that folk cultures are sometimes slow to arise to a revolutionary cause. Hence, it might not be wise to expect Indians to immediately address the matters at hand. But the people to the east in Guatemala, for the most part, are not Indians; hence the emphasis on that area. Other reasons as well. Why not work for a peaceful development of the Indian? We are doing this. But we have reasons to doubt our effectiveness. Labor leaders have been killed in the Coban and Huehuetenango areas. Organization of labor is associated with the regimes of Arevelo and Arbenz, hence is always suspect of 'communism.'[9] Our coops in Ixcan and the Peten have been destroyed.

"And what can we say of communism? A polycentric movement. Surely having a unity under stress. We see its hybrids in Yugoslavia, Poland and Cuba, as well as the deep differences between China and Russia. It has been referred to as a dictatorship of the proletariat and certainly there is great room for improvement in even the most humane of these countries.

"But the rightists, the oligarchy who say Latin America is not ready for democracy, they speak lovingly of the days of Jorge Ubico, and say that we need dictatorship in Latin America.[10] If this is so, we should not look for that dictatorship in one person who can be easily removed, but rather as an institution hopefully managed by people who care about the masses and who will put social development first and economic development second. Technical development will follow when the basic needs of people are put in first place. Any system of majority rule can be categorized as a dictatorship over an unfortunate minority.

"I had an interesting discussion with Padre Alejandro. He mentioned the despair present in the institutional Church, which made it necessary to have a year dedicated to faith. Alejandro states that despair is to the right. He expressed the need for prophets at this time. This is the exodus from slavery. What was an idol to the Jews? An idol is a god that does not liberate the people. Out of slavery into the promised land.

"Alejandro categorized many of the existing leadership programs within the supervision of the Church as designed for leaders in underdevelopment (lideres en subdesarrollo) or micro-leaders. What we need are macro-leaders.

"According to Alejandro, fidelity to the past implies a complete break with the past. Conformity to the past is to be a traitor to the lessons of the past, to the dynamism of the past, for example, a religious man who wants to live as a novice when he has an apostolate in the secular world. Changes will come in the Latin American Revolution, said Padre Alejandro, once enough myth (mito) is formed. For example, Che is now a myth. Camilo Torres is now a myth.[11]

"Alejandro is clearly expressing the birth of a theology that is free of the weight of past centuries. He refers to incarnation as entering completely into the life of the community up to the ultimate consequences, which, of course, may include crucifixion. This is a matter of entering into the hopes of the poor, and to go on with them to the end. We do not give the poor our hopes, our desires, but we proceed in the search, and the effort to achieve their hopes, their desires, their values.

"My visit with Padre Alejandro was indeed a privilege. He is here in Guatemala unknown to the government. Should they be aware of the presence of this revolutionary priest, he would certainly either be expelled immediately or possibly assassinated.

"Continuing with the thoughts of Alejandro: We do not enter into the incarnation of a community without retaining our own character. This is the lesson of the Word. He did not cease to be God, but entered completely into our way of life. We do not have to cease to be intellectuals or technical experts in order to enter into the lives of the poor.

"But we must be the bridge, the ones who are the synthesis between the groups, that is, between campesinos (peasants) and finqueros (landed farmers) and the other elements of society. A prophet does not necessarily speak among his own. He frequently does not even belong to the group among whom he is prophesying. Prophets among workers have not necessarily been from the working class. Organizers of revolutions are rarely from the destitute classes.

"We do not have a lesson for the poor and another lesson for the rich. We have a lesson for the human race. To be human, to be a person, to understand our dignity regardless of what we have. To understand what we are. The Old Testament Jews lived in a desert and fought for their liberation from slavery in Egypt. The march of mankind includes this desire for liberation. The institutional Church does not give us this mandate. The mandate is from natural law, the law of conscience. Secularization is to understand the hopes and desires of the human race in the secular order as part of the incarnation.[12] We must be incarnate and secular.

"It is revolutions themselves that will change church structures. Political changes will come and the institutional Church will follow these changes on a worldwide scale. In the New Testament, arming oneself for war is a matter of laying aside all unnecessary baggage. We quote several instances:

> For again, what king marching to war against another king would not first sit down and consider whether with 10,000 men he could stand up to the other who advanced against him with 20,000? If not, then while the other king was still a long way off, he would send envoys to sue for peace. So in the same way, none of you can be my disciple unless he gives up all his possessions. (Luke 14; 31-33)[13]

> Or if no one can be sure which call the trumpet has sounded, who will be ready for the attack? (Corinthians 1; 14, 8)[14]

> Is there any need to say more? There is not time for me to give an account of Gideon, Barak, Samson, Jephthat, or David, Samuel and the prophets. These were men who, through faith, conquered kingdoms, did what is right, and earned the promises. They could keep a lion's mouth shut, put out blazing fires, and emerge unscathed from battle. They were weak people who were given strength to be brave in war and drive back foreign invaders. Some came back to their lives from the dead, by resurrection; and others submitted to torture, refusing release so that they would rise again to a better life. Some had to bear being pilloried or flogged, or even chained up in prison. They were stoned or sawn in half, or beheaded; they were homeless and dressed

in the skins of sheep and goats; they were penniless and were given nothing but ill treatment. They were too good for the world and they went out to live in deserts and mountains and in caves and ravines. These are all heroes of faith, but they did not receive what was promised, since God had made provisions for us to have something better, and they were not to reach perfection except with us.

With so many witnesses in a great cloud on every side of us, we too, then, should throw off everything that hinders us, especially the sin that clings so evenly, and keep running steadily in the race we have started. Let us not lose sight of Jesus, who leads us in our faith and brings it to perfection: for the sake of the joy which was still in the future, he endured the cross, disregarding the shamefulness of it, and from now on, has taken his place at the right of God's throne. Think of the way he stood such opposition from sinners and then you will not give up for want of courage. In the fight against sin, you have not yet had to keep fighting to the point of death. (Hebrews 11; 32-40, 12; 1-4)[15]

And Jesus answered them, 'Take care that no one deceives you; because many will come using my name and saying, I am the Christ, and they will deceive many. You will hear of wars and rumors of war. Do not be alarmed, for this is something that must happen. But the end will not be yet. For nation will fight against nation, and kingdom against kingdom. There will be famines and earthquakes here and there. All this is only the beginning of the birth pangs.

'Then they will hand you over to be tortured and put to death; and you will be hated by all the nations on account of my name. And then many will fall away; men will betray one another and hate one another. False prophets will arise; they will deceive many, and with the increase of lawlessness, love in most people will grow cold. But the person who stands firm to the end will be saved.

'This good news of the kingdom will be proclaimed to the whole world as a witness to all nations. And then the end will come.'" (Matthew 24; 4-14)[16]

Revolutionary Decisions

One of the characteristics of liberation theology and its development in Central America was reliance upon Scriptural literature. While living in the developed world, it was easy to have access to so-called modern theological texts, most of which were a monument to casuistry. Traveling light in the h ghlands of Guatemala, it was difficult to consider carrying more than one book. That book, of course, was the Bible. All of us from the so-called developed world were struck by the purity of Biblical literature when read in the context of the poor.

The good news about which Jesus speaks is good news to the poor. There is no way the poor are going to discuss good news in their base communities, and in their reflections and praxis on the Bible, without discussing their right to eat, their right to health, their right to an education, their right to land, their right to live as human beings.

It seemed strange to us to imagine that in the developed world and in the urban religious societies we had known it was possible to discuss the Gospel without talking about the social problem. This reality only goes to prove the stultifying nature of western urban theological development.

In November 1967, while trying to reflect on the formal incorporation of the cursillos into a clandestine organization, I received a visit from a member of the Junta Directiva of the FAR. The visitor, who arrived late at night at the rectory, was speaking as an official representative of the rebel forces. They had been aware for some time that the unarmed work of the guerrillas of peace or the Cursillos de Capacitación Social was becoming a target for the Guatemalan military. It was not unusual for members of the FAR to arrive while cursillos were taking place and ask to address the participants. It was customary for these armed rebels to express nothing but admiration for the dedication, the organization and the effectiveness of the cursillos, but while they expressed such appreciation, they expressed their confidence that the organization had no future in Central America. They observed that our organization was a sitting duck. We were living in a vast illiteracy drive. The most intelligent, reflective, and cultural voices of Central America were being silenced. Illiteracy was not an accident in Guatemala; it was the objective of the Guatemalan government. Literacy was called a communist plot. Health education was called a communist plot. Land reform was called a communist plot. Christian base communities including the Cursillos de Capacitación Social were nothing but communist plots, according to the government.

There was always a solid ring of truth to the logic and presentations given by the rebels as they spoke in our rural gatherings. But that evening's visitor to the rectory made more than an observation; he made a statement of the utmost urgency. This particular rebel, Comandante Juan, certainly did not conform to the stereotypical North American image of a "terrorist." Juan had worked for years in social services directly with parishes in the Indian regions of Guatemala. He was a student of enormous academic achievement. His studies for his doctorate were terminated because of his participation in the revolution. Juan's message to me in my capacity as national advisor of the Cursillos de Capacitación Social, was to at once enter into dialogue and formulate just what the relationship would be between the rebels and the cursillos.

Many students were leaving the cursillo program and simply going into training as rebels. The conversation between myself and Comandante Juan took most of the night and it was obvious that both the rebels themselves and the church programs were in a process of change. The rebels had a foco mentality, that is, strategy based on conducting small units of opposition in the mountain areas. They were aware of their poor communications with the indigenous people.[17]

The Church organizations, on the other hand, had excellent relationships with the Indian people and were certainly not isolated focos. Comandante Juan surprised me at the opening of the conversation by saying, "The revolution in the Church will begin with the revolution in Guatemala."

It became clear to me that the rebels were not looking for chaplains, and certainly couldn't see clergymen as being apart from other members. They were not inviting us as clergy to participate on the fringe of the organization, as the typical Catholic chaplain or any chaplain in the U.S. armed forces. They were speaking of equality among all members; all members are participants. In speaking of the institutional Church, Comandante Juan expressed himself with great reverence. He said, "We are going to be very hard on the institution of the Church because we want a Church that is more pure, a Church that represents the teachings of Jesus in all their simplicity."

A journal entry for the same period reads: "It appears that we priests have a duty to remain in our place. We are vicars of the Good Shepherd, who would not flee as the mercenaries did in the moment of danger. But the Good Shepherd remains in his place, ready to give his life for his people. Indeed, Jesus ordered his Apostles to go from city to city in the case of personal persecution. This is different than the case of war or revolution, where we are concerned about all of the people. In this latter case, the leader must remain with the people. Surely if all of the people decided to become exiles, the Shepherd might leave with the multitude. But he, as shepherd, must not attempt to save himself individually, and certainly not with a minority of opportunists or fearful people."

We discussed the serious problem of taking up arms at length. I asked the Comandante what would happen if members of the FAR demonstrated a love of violence. His response: "We would expel them from the organization. We are not interested in people who love violence." When I asked him if there had been abuses in the organization, he was quick to acknowledge their lack of perfection. He was quick to speak of their errors. And he added with great seriousness, "If you know of a way that we can free our people through some other process, please tell me what it is."

As the conversation continued, to my utter surprise, I realized that Comandante Juan was not simply speaking of members of our organization joining his organization. He was speaking of something entirely new. His concept was that of the formation of a new and autonomous Christian guerrilla front. It was his opinion that many members of the Cursillos de Capacitación Social would be inclined to participate in such a front, and would not be equally inclined to join the FAR. Comandante Juan was aware that to be successful, a revolutionary venture required communion with the culture in which it was born. He was also aware of the reflection of Che Guevara, quoted in the introduction:

> Christians must definitively choose the revolution, and especially on our continent where the Christian faith is so important among the masses. When Christians begin to give an integral revolutionary witness, the Latin American Revolution will be invincible. Until now, Christians have permitted their doctrines to be manipulated by reactionaries.[18]

By December of 1967, events moved with stunning speed. The leadership of the Centro de Capacitación Social was listed by the secret police of Guatemala. This meant they either had to disappear on their own accord or they might be "disappeared" by the secret police themselves. We began to shuttle leaders out of Guatemala. Some were brought to the border with El Salvador. Some were brought to the border with Mexico. Some left by air. But all knew there would be a place to meet in Mexico in order to regroup and organize a Christian revolutionary front.

My specific personal participation was still unclear. On November 28, 1967, I made the following journal entry:

"And now a question, why not go to the States and shout out the facts in every media possible? TV, radio, newspapers. My thought was that while in the U.S. I could reach people from coast to coast. The giant development of public opinion in the U.S.A. against U.S. intervention in Guatemala could save millions of lives and make possible a popular revolution, a re-structuring of Latin America.

"This priestly and prophetic work would result in opposition from the power structure of Maryknoll. But there is a conscience problem here. If one can cry out and save lives by developing pressures contrary to intervention—it is worth the effort.

"But one must protect the Church even in this circumstance. One must obey the local bishops in matters of suspension from celebration of mass, etc. Only in the area of civil disobedience to human, ecclesiastical, and civil law should the prophet proceed. This is his vision. The error of many modern prophets is to throw out everything. The prophet should receive his suspensions, excommunications, and prohibitions with a certain grace. He should abide with all of the directives he can.

"But the prophet's vision, what Habakkuk saw—was it not the conclusion of an intellect and will functioning before the problems of his day?"

> How long, Yahweh, am I to cry for help while you will not listen; to cry 'oppression!' and you will not save?
> Why do you set injustice before me, and why do you look on where there is tyranny? Outrage and violence, this is all I see, all is contention, and discord flourishes.
> And so the law loses its hold, and justice never shows itself. Yes, the wicked man gets the better of the upright, and so justice is seen to be distorted.
> Cast your eyes over the nations, look, and be amazed, astounded, for I am doing something in your own days that you would not believe if you were told of it.
> For I am stirring up the Chaldeans, that fierce and fiery people who march miles across country to seize the homes of others.
> A people feared and dreaded, from their might proceeds their right, their greatness." (Habakkuk 1;2-7)[19]

The role of the prophet is to speak in front of the problems and injustices of his time: 'Jerusalem, Jerusalem, you that kill the prophets and stone those who are sent to you!'" (Matthew 23; 37)[20]

In my diary entry for November 27, 1967 I wrote:

"I understand the possibility of temporary laicization, that is of two years, is now easy to obtain...But the work of announcing impending dangers is imminently prophetic and priestly, hence why request laicization to do such a deeply priestly work? But the power structure of the institution, for example, Maryknoll, and local bishops will doubtless intervene. Hence the witness of their intervention is necessary in order to prove their error.

"Also, we see the necessity of priests to be able to operate on a national or international level in the manner of a Billy Graham. Yes, it is a prophetic role. 'Whom shall I send?' asked the Lord. 'Lo, here I am, send me!'

"But where are the issues upon which we should prophesy? The role of the United States in international affairs, especially in Latin

America. Conscience. Civil disobedience within the Church. Civil disobedience within society. Ecclesiastical teachings on marriage and birth control. Excommunicated Catholics. Obedience to the Church. Obedience to Christ. Protestant-Catholic relations. Freedom of action. Parochial limitations. Married clergy. Work for salary. The war in Vietnam and Central America. De-mythologizing society. The needs of Latin America. The impact of guerrilla warfare on the hemisphere. Pax Americana. Colleges. Love of the Church. Refusal to resign from the Church or to request laicization. Allegiance to the Pope; primacy of honor. Fidelity to the prophetic role. Money. Catholic schools. The election of bishops. Absence of the prophetic role in the Church. Freedom. Idol worship. Civil laws of the Church. The development of a moral theology. Freedom to think, to work, and to act. Asking reconciliation and accepting reconciliation. "In short, systematizing love.

"This appears to be the last chance for the United States. We do not have to be destroyed. We have hope. We do not have to be Nazis. We do not need genocide. We have time but time is short. Resistance movements are essential, including violence against things, like the Boston tea party or acts against draft records. Better to burn paper than to burn people. A message to the youth: do not go. Do not fight in an immoral war."

Later, in my journal of December 12, 1967 I wrote:

"I did not expect to be leading a procession of thousands of people through Guatemala City on this feast day, the Day of Our Lady of Guadalupe, but that is what happened. I was asked to substitute for the Guatemalan priest who was to have this honor. May this novena of Our Lady of Guadalupe be a source of grace and decision.

"I am beginning these exercises believing that many of the forms are outdated. Firecrackers, processions, and even the paraliturgical prayers and devotions. The use of the sacrament of penance is appalling. So much better to have a community exercise. The individualized system here seems to be clogged with deaf old ladies, and children and men who want to celebrate a social function, wedding, cumpleaños (birthday) or quinceaños (15th birthday) of their daughters.

"Spoke at length to one of the Basque fathers about the place of civil disobedience in the church. He was very much in accord that it has a place and that we must be ready to act in conscience. May we bury the canonical mentality; give to priests the independence of free men, earning their own living and giving adult witness to the Lord. May we not waste time with excessive doctrinal considerations which become a mass of words without meaning. May God guide us to love the Church, to reform the Church, to enter into the service of the world and no longer be marginal to society, nor simply a source of consolation to the aged. We must enter into the true points of tension in the world as Christ did.

"What are the signs of the marginal nature of the institutional Church? It's general desire that its priests act under direction from above rather than to encourage individual initiative. It's top heavy authority. Men with no professional competence given authority to make decisions in areas of technical domain, for example, social work. Mass stipends as a source of income rather than constructive work making many priests parasitic to the society. Folkways, anti-intellectuality. Legalism, *ipso facto* application of mortal sin to people. Over-sacramentalization in place of Christian action. Pious silliness; sisters taught to save five cents by sending letters in person rather than mailing the letter thereby costing ten dollars in effort, and wasting years and millions of dollars in apostolic foolishness, for example, training schools for the rich, lack of attention to the poor of the world, lack of attention to corrupt structures, especially governments. Individualistic concepts of sin and salvation in place of awareness of social sins and institutional evils. Clerical garb. The necessity for many to leave the institution in order to speak their mind. Weak, spineless, dull people in high places. Almost without exception, men performing meaningful, effective, and dynamic apostolates are either simply tolerated or punished by the power structures. I was so moved by the intellectual honesty of my father on his recent visit to Guatemala. Here is a man of enormous professional competence in his mid-70s, a judge of the Superior Court of the State of California, within a few days of observing the misery of Guatemala speaks as a Republican of over fifty years standing and says, the night before he returns to the United States, 'If I lived here I would join the guerrillas.'"

It is difficult to reconstruct the pace of activities of December 1967. Students were still scattered throughout the mountains of Huehuetenango. It was necessary to pull them all together and to thank God that some ninety of them were able to regroup without the loss of anyone. The coming together was celebrated by a dance. Prior to the dance there was a collective celebration of the sacrament of Penance. During the dance there was a constant and continuous exchange of information among the dancers: which of the leaders were leaving the country; who were they going to leave with; where were they going to reassemble; who was still safe in living openly in Guatemala; what was happening to the priests and sisters involved in the movement?

During the dance itself the Assistant Superior of the Maryknoll appeared to speak to me. He had an airline ticket in his hand and told me that I was to be on board a flight scheduled for Christmas Eve, 1967. The decision from on-high that many of us priests and sisters should leave the country immediately was a product of the United States embassy and the Ambassador, John Gordon Mein. The Ambassador, using diplomatic phraseology, stated that he could "no longer protect us." I have seen and heard this phrase in many contexts since that time. It is sad to know that the Ambassador himself was unable to be protected and died in an exchange of gunfire between his body guards and rebels of the FAR some months later.

I was personally amazed at the fury expressed by the Maryknoll Superior in Guatemala. He had asked me to meet him at the Las Vegas Restaurant in Guatemala City, and it was there that he stated that he was aware I was not telling him all that was transpiring with my movement. I was not aware that I was under any mandate to do this, but as he continued in his fury he stated that if I did not tell him all that was transpiring he would attack me physically and I would be "spitting out my teeth like Chiclets."

Fortunately, his Assistant Superior was there as a witness to this exchange. After his threat of physical violence against me I responded that I thought he had made a mistake in challenging me because I had been trained extensively in hand-to-hand combat and any such attack on my person might be to his detriment. Upon reflection, I realized that this was the first near physical conflict in which I had been engaged in decades.

The Superior seemed shocked by my response, as did his assistant, but they should both have been aware that the threat was initiated by the Superior himself.

My remaining days in Guatemala were spent in secreting the files of the Centro de Capacitacion Social, in secreting the known student leaders and helping many of them to get out of the country, and in organizing some final details regarding the material administration of the student center. When the final, predictable police and military attack came upon our headquarters in Guatemala City we were overjoyed that the building was empty. After careful consultation with the leadership of the movement and my own personal reflections, I determined to be on that Christmas Eve plane in order to return to the United States and inform the media of the realities of Guatemala.

—4—
Back to the USA
"You will learn the truth and the truth will make you free."
John 8, 32

Leaving Maryknoll: Preaching In The Press

There was a good deal of re-entry shock on returning to the United States after my experiences in Guatemala. I arrived at the Maryknoll headquarters in New York just in time for Christmas midnight mass. In the procession of priests was the Superior General of Maryknoll. I greeted him with, "Merry Christmas, Father General." His response was "Good evening." I knew I was in trouble.

The Superior General indicated some time after that midnight mass that he was too angry to speak to me, hence I waited until December 29, 1967 to have my first meeting with him. When the meeting finally took place I entered his office with a notebook and said, "I understand you wanted to talk to me." He said, "No, I did not want to talk to you." Then he said, "You have been making a damn fool out of yourself." I began to write in my notebook and he said, "Stop writing!" A series of threats followed: Various threats of suspension, three invitations to leave the Maryknoll Society, frequent statements that there was no work for me in the society. Ultimately he assigned me to a building in Pennsylvania which was empty and due to be sold. I left the meeting thinking about the fact that there was no charge, no hearing, no defense, no dialogue, and no humanity. If what he said were true, that he had no job for me, then I must certainly find my own job.

I had planned to communicate with the Superior General about how I am canonically responsible for the students and others who had to flee from Guatemala, that my written mandate from the Archbishop of Guatemala was neither rescinded nor withdrawn, that my flock was in flight and in hiding from murderous and deadly secret police and military, and that I had reason to be here on their behalf and to ask others if they could assist in the welfare of my flock. But it was not possible to communicate any of these things.

Various priests at the center house of Maryknoll heard about my curious assignment to an empty building in Pennsylvania and interceded on my behalf with the irritated Superior General. The General conceded that instead of going to the empty building I should go to Hawaii.

63

I asked the Superior General if it would be all right to pursue my doctoral studies at my own expense. His answer was no. The National Council of Churches requested my presence for a year as a lecturer on Central American affairs. Permission was denied. I asked for permission to attend a National Meeting on Latin America to be conducted in St. Louis within the coming month.

The Superior General finally conceded that I might spend a few days at the Latin America Conference prior to reporting for my assignment in Hawaii. I went to St. Louis and there I found the Catholic and secular press most receptive to my comments about the actual situation in Central America. I was under threat of automatic suspension if I did not arrive in Hawaii prior to midnight by February 1, 1968. At this point the legalisms were becoming somewhat humorous. My suspension or non-suspension depended on the speed of the trade winds over the Pacific Ocean.

Arriving at 11:58 p.m., the moment when the wheels touched down in Oahu, the assembled awaiting priests assured me I was not suspended. We proceeded to the Maryknoll house in Honolulu, where I was informed that I was not to speak about Latin America, not to write about Latin America, not to engage in student works, not to engage in social works, to forget everything that had happened in Latin America, and to direct my attention to my new assignment.

While I was in a state of near physical exhaustion and relished the thought of spending many weeks of rest on the Hawaiian beaches, I concluded it was not possible to remain under these circumstances. The following morning the *Washington Post* called and asked for more details about the Latin Vietnam I had described in St. Louis. In speaking from the Maryknoll house in Honolulu, it was obvious to me that such activities would not be tolerated, especially in light of the orders I had received.

I reflected on the fact that what I had been given was actually a mandate to leave the Maryknoll Society. It would not be morally possible for me to remain silent on the reality of Central America, especially in view of my responsibilities to those who were now in hiding. Should I have accepted the mandate of Maryknoll to remain silent, I pictured myself saying morning mass and playing golf six days a week. Such conduct might have been rewarded as obedience. But to me it was simply a temptation, and a temptation I did not care to give in to. I asked about the departure of the next plane for the States and informed the Superior in Honolulu that I would leave in order to clarify my position with the Superior General. I had been in Honolulu less than 24 hours before departure. I proceeded directly to Washington, D.C., informed the Maryknoll headquarters of my whereabouts and activities and spent hours with the editorial board of the *Washington Post*. My first syndicated column was released by the

Washington Post on Sunday, February 4, 1968, under the title, "A Priest in Guatemala." At the risk of interrupting the saga of relations with Maryknoll, it may be instructive to reproduce a piece of that article here. It is more exact than my recollections would be and, on re-reading, it has a relevance today as well.

"The Central American Republic of Guatemala may well be the Vietnam of tomorrow. American activities so far in the smoldering Guatemalan civil war suggest that the United States, in betrayal of its highest ideals, is preparing to take on the futile task of commanding the tides of freedom to roll back.

"Guatemala smells like South Vietnam did a few years ago. There are the same United States military advisers by the hundreds, the same corrupt power structure, the same fear of communism to the point of paranoia, the same group of peasants weak in themselves but firmly determined that no foreigner is going to overcome them on their land.

"Those who lead the Guatemalan revolution look at the United States involvement in Vietnam and say: 'You Americans, with a half million troops, with bombs, with napalm, with an air force, with the best military expertise in the world, with the finest technical aid, have not been able to contain the situation in half of one small Asian country. What is going to happen when you are confronted with ten Latin American countries? If you learn your lesson from Vietnam— we might say, if you repent of Vietnam—you will not be destroyed. If you repeat the Vietnam experience in Guatemala, in Colombia, in Bolivia, in Brazil, in Mexico, in Peru, we Latin Americans maintain that there will not be a United States.'

"As a North American priest, I believe that this insight of the Latin American, both the intellectual and the common-sense peasant, is correct. Those who guide United States foreign policy have found the formula for the destruction of the greatest nation in the world. The formula is to try to contain or to destroy valid popular revolutions. We cannot do it. The lesson of our history should teach us that raw power cannot be set against the will of whole populations.

"In Guatemala, the United States is standing militarily behind an oligarchy of two percent of the Guatemalan people who possess eighty percent of the land and resultant power.

"We Americans have supplied the army with weapons, with training, with helicopters, with planes. We have helped the national police to hire new personnel and provided them new carbines, so that pairs of policemen are now found on every street corner. We have bought the police cars for the secret police.

"In a very real way, the Guatemalan army is our army. If it were at the service of the people, it might be encouraging to know that we had staffed an instrument of law and order in Latin America. But this army is in the service of corruption. It is in the service of a society in which most people are hungry.

"Over half the Guatemalan people are suffering from malnutrition. A wage of fifty cents a day in Guatemala is above average, but meat is forty cents a pound and eggs fifty to sixty cents a dozen. This means that people don't eat and children die unnecessarily. Of the 70,000 a year who die in Guatemala, 30,000 are children. Guatemala's child mortality rate is forty times that of the United States.

"During my fifteen months in Guatemala, I was the national director of the Cursillos de Capacitacion Social; in English, Workshops on the Social Question. At the National University of Guatemala, we operated what might be called a 'center of social awareness.'

"In Guatemala, university students total about .4 of a percent of the population. This tiny minority is extremely important and rather vociferous. In our program in the National University we started the students off with eight days of work, study, eat, sleep. During the eight days we studied capitalism, socialism, Marxism, communism, papal encyclicals on social questions, sociological data on Guatemala, possible solutions to the Guatemalan phenomenon. On the course's eighth day we invited the student into the field to meet the farmer and to work with him in understanding what we had discussed.

"The students, working mostly on weekends, discussed with the peasants such concepts as the dignity of man, the common good, community, the right to organize peasants' leagues, that is, farmers unions.

"When a break occurred in the regular school schedule, we invited the students to direct six-week courses in literacy, hygiene and health.

"During our last six-week program, we received one of many accusations that came our way. Someone mentioned to me that he had heard from the army, from the far right, that we were about to begin an armed revolution in Huehuetenango. I said it would be easy to prove the falsity of such an accusation by going up to Huehuetenango and seeing what the ninety students were doing. We invited the mayor, the governor, various high-ranking military officers to see the closing of the program.

"Those who went up there saw that there wasn't even a slingshot.

"I am called a communist in Guatemala. So is anyone who is interested in the organization of labor, in seeing the peasant earn more than forty cents a day, in a just division of the lands—anyone who spends too much time concerned about the very poor.

"I have been told by wealthy people: 'We will stop you.'

"After the wealthy charged my friends and me with being communists, they charged that we were plotting armed revolution. This second accusation was really the most dangerous and it led several students to flee for their lives.

"Church money was given to various students to help them get out of the country, and I think that the accusation that the Melvilles had used church money for other than church purposes is false. I think they used church money to help students flee the country for their lives, and I think that would always be a good place to use church money. It was urgent that these students leave because they would be shot down without a hearing by the secret police. That's how Guatemala now operates.

"We'd better get used to socialistic states in Latin America, because we're not likely to see anything more mild than Mexican socialism, and other solutions will probably be farther left.

"We don't want Cuba or any other country pointing missiles at us. But neither can we expect to determine what kind of government other countries are going to have. This implies a great change in the psychological relationship of the United States to Latin America. All through our history we have acted as if the Latin nations were our colonies.

"The sooner we learn these independent nations are not our colonies, the fewer guerrillas we are going to have in the mountains.

"The guerrilla is not just a loud-mouthed ruffian. My image of him is a soft-spoken, well-read, dedicated person who has reluctantly made the decision, backed up by a majority of Latin American sociologists, that the only way to change the current power structure in Latin America is violence.

"Frequently the guerrilla comes to this conclusion because he is a Christian. The development of the Christian mystique in the armed movement in Latin America may be the catalytic agent that will bring about revolution in these countries more rapidly than we had imagined.

"I believe the well-read student can say honestly the status quo is so intolerably violent that it is killing my brother: my brother is suffering as a result of the institutionalized violence in which he lives. He is dying because he doesn't eat. He is dying because he doesn't have land. He is dying because he cannot organize his labor. He is dying intellectually because he has no schools.

"To take a nonviolent position in the face of such violence is to approve of violence. The Latin American guerrilla of a Christian temper, taught by Pope Paul's Christmas message, agrees that Christianity is not pacifism and believes that the witness of his fighting is necessary at this time.

"I find that the guerrilla frequently has the New Testament in his pocket. I recall one saying to me that he had lost eighty of his friends in one year and that this had made him very sad. But he said that Jesus had told us the seed had to fall into the ground and die or it would remain by itself alone. He felt that he and his friends were the seed of a new order that was coming to Guatemala.

"There is a great prophetic ring about so many of the things that the guerrilla says. One told me the revolution in the church would begin in Guatemala. He said, 'We are going to be very hard on the church, but I think that we are going to have a church that is more pure, a church that is more primitive in the good sense of the word, and I think that the ecclesiastical revolution will begin here in Guatemala.'

"The commitment of Guatemalan intellectuals is now beginning to reach the uneducated. The peasant has a catalyst of revolution in his hand, the transistor radio. He realizes something is wrong with his life and he knows that it can be better. He knows that the goods and services of society do not reach him. He is willing to fight rather than deteriorate.

"I am a patriot. It sickens me to see my country on the wrong side in Guatemala. I think the United States is the greatest country in the world, and I don't want to see it on a self-destruction course. These new five, six, seven, eight new Vietnams that could erupt in Latin America would be the end of the United States because we would find that our boys wouldn't go.

"The fact that two priests, Fathers Art and Tom Melville and Sister Marian Peter—some of my closest friends—entered into the Latin American revolution directly does not surprise me. Their act is a valid witness for the church in Latin America. Things are that bad.

"In his encyclical on development (Populorum Progressio), Pope Paul states that violent revolutions generally beget new evil and are not to be encouraged. But he qualifies the generalization, excluding revolts "where there is manifest long standing tyranny which would do great damage to fundamental personal rights and dangerous harm to the common good of the country.

"If there is anywhere in the world where such tyranny has persisted, it is Latin America. Centuries have not been time enough to bring development any further than selfishness, individualism and 19th Century buccaneer capitalism.

"I think that the Melvilles and Sister Marian Peter will one day be looked upon as among the great heroes of the church in this century, because they helped point up the horrors of the intervention of power politics into small, weak nations.

"I think what they're doing is going to result in many people having a better way of life and is going to bring attention to the great errors that the United States makes by muscling its way into Latin American countries.

"Hence, if I think there's any message from all this for the United States, I would say that we should discontinue our vast military aid to Latin American countries.

"We could give our attention to projects of social betterment. Then also we could understand that we are opposing currents of thought and desire in Latin America that are already formed and growing. Those currents are not specifically communistic, but with our current posture, only communistic nations are taking advantage of these currents of thought and desire.

"Contemporary religious thought, taught by the Second Vatican Council, has brought us much closer to the revolutionary mind. Before the Council it was common to think that as missionaries we should arrive in a foreign land with desires, hopes and goals, and give these hopes, desires and goals to the people.

"But a better understanding of the Incarnation teaches me that my job is to arrive in a foreign land and to enter into the hopes, the desires and the anxieties of the people, even unto their ultimate consequences.

"In days to come the word 'missionary' will be clothed with deeper meaning. Alan Paton says well what mission is not: 'Love without justice is a Christian impossibility, and can only be practiced by those who have divorced religion from life, who dismiss a concern for justice as politics and who fear social change much more than they fear God.'"

From my article perhaps it will be clear why at this point I was convinced that my work with the media in the United States was indeed my current apostolate. Perhaps my hopes for how much impact this witness could have were inflated, but in any event, I was sure of my course. I continued to inform Maryknoll headquarters of my whereabouts and my activities, but was simply told to return to Hawaii. In view of the fact that the conditions of the assignment were considered by me to be completely immoral, I found an apartment in Washington and began to earn my own keep. On February 28, 1968 the *National Catholic News Service* released an article claiming that 102 Maryknoll missionaries in Guatemala repudiated the revolutionary actions taken by myself and the other priests, together with Sister Marian Peter:

> ...emphasizing Maryknoll's apolitical role in Guatemala, the letter to [the Superior General] Father John J. McCormack, M.M., said:
>
> "Statements given to the United States press by priests of this society who were recently expelled from Guatemala have tried to gain stature for their very personal 'Christian witness' and have cornered the front pages of the press around the world.
>
> "We want to make clearly known that those statements reflect no more than their own very personal points of view, which from no standpoint can be assumed to promote the official opinion of the Maryknoll Society.

"The erroneous opinions as well as the thinking adopted by
Thomas and Arthur Melville, by the ex-Sister Marian Peter
and Blase Bonpane, are completely foreign to the Maryknoll community in Guatemala since they, against our
norms, took active part in the internal affairs of the
country."

Commenting that the action of their four former co-workers
was "naive, showing a complete ignorance of the realities of
this country," the 102 signers of the letter said that the
four's involvement in politics, because it was contrary to
Article 66 of the Constitution of the Republic of Guatemala,
forced their expulsion from the country.

The letter added that "this painful incident has concerned
us beyond measure, since it has given rise to a misunder-
standing about the work of the 102 Maryknoll priests,
Brothers and Sisters who still work in and identify themselves with this generous country, asking in exchange no
more than that their vigil become a direct spiritual and
material benefit to the country.

"With all our heart we pledge ourselves to continue working
for the welfare of this country, of which we have become so
much a part. In spite of the problem which we have had, we
place our complete faith and confidence in the right judg-
ment of those people of Guatemala who know of our work
through the last quarter-century..."

Controversy over the Fathers Melville, brothers from New-
ton, Mass., over Father Bonpane and over Sister Marian
Peter Bradford erupted after their cooperation with Guatemala revolutionaries became known. Ordered to return to
Maryknoll headquarters in New York, only Father Bonpane showed up.

As a result, the Melvilles were suspended from the priesthood.

Soon after, Sister Marian Peter married Father Thomas
Melville, incurring automatic excommunication for both.

The three Melvilles have continued their pro-revolutionary
work from Mexico while publishing several articles and
statements defending their activities here...

In the years which have transpired, I have had the opportunity to
question many, if not most, of the 102 Maryknollers in Guatemala at
that time. I have yet to meet one missionary who has acknowledged
signing the statement. Hence, the very honesty and origin of the
statement is in question.

By March 4, 1968, an article appeared in the *Washington Post*
which reported that "The Maryknoll missionary order announced

yesterday that the Rev. Blase Bonpane, one of seven missionaries withdrawn from Guatemala in December for working with communist guerrillas, had 'unilaterally disassociated himself' from the Order's work. However, Father Bonpane indicated that Maryknoll had itself suspended him because he would not report for a second time to a new assignment in Honolulu."

During March of 1968, it became increasingly clear to me that my role in the United States, as planned in Guatemala, was a correct one and that unfortunately it would not be possible for me to continue this work within the context of Maryknoll. My Washington office was deluged with requests from universities around the United States and from the press, television, and radio.

In contrast to the message of the document which was alleged to have been signed by all Maryknollers in Guatemala, efforts in El Salvador, Nicaragua, Panama, and the South American countries led to an episcopal conference of the Latin American Bishops at Medellin in Colombia in 1968. Conference documents are available in their entirety and give clear justification for the movements of people away from misery and toward social justice.

Some journal entries written during this period follow.

Revolutionary Reflections

"This appears to be a curtailment of freedom of speech and that freedom includes preaching the word of God. Personally, I am incapable of responding to threats as valid motives to thwart the Christian conscience."

"People in the States have a right to know what is happening in Guatemala. I see the same advisors in Guatemala that were the prelude to the slaughter in Vietnam. I see the same arrogance of power; the same blind opposition to a valid revolution of the destitute. The same napalm, the same previews of horror."

"In the site of this horrible vision, to accept the ecclesiastical penalty of suspension is a very small matter compared to the necessity of a witness against the immorality of U.S. involvement in Vietnam and Guatemala."

"Many of my fellow Maryknollers realized that at this juncture of history these tensions are not only necessary but quite productive."

"May the words of the founder, Father James Anthony Walsh, now have new meaning for us: 'We must be bigger than the society.'"

"There was a time when U.S. interests and Christianity seemed to coincide. That time is gone."

"The Church in the United States seems to be more closely aligned with capitalism than it is with Christianity."

"Morality demands that errors be brought to light and faith demands that we set out like Abraham, not knowing exactly where we are going."

"Conclusions may easily be drawn. Order is desirable and to be sought after, but must never stand as an obstacle to the truth. Charity demands authenticity, the role of prophet is always marginal to society, ecclesiastical and civil. The role of prophet is neither to be common nor sought after. Some few have to accept it in conscience. Let their words be their acceptance or condemnation."

"The institutional Church is not reflecting the life of the spirit. Rather it is frequently the pharasee. Charismatic voices are tolerated at best or silenced. Unfortunately the institutional Church is where the money is. There are many superb people in the institution of the Church, but many of them have become "good guys" and have been unfaithful to their mission. They are like doctors who don't want to hurt their patients, who choose to avoid surgery rather than cause suffering, and who watch the patient die. The privacy of many priests, Brothers and Sisters is violated in the name of obedience, loyalty, etc., but mediocrity is a safe ground and is rampant."

"Fear of trouble is more intense than fear of evil and this is a current sin of the Church."

"Who am I? I am a priest with a prophetic calling. I asked neither laicization nor separation from the Church. I seek neither schism nor heresy."

"Priests, brothers and sisters should remain faithful to the institution if they can do so in conscience, be a part of the changes, help to avoid the ugly schism which can easily arrive in the Church."

"Realize that the Church must bring good news to the poor. We are not doing this in the United States. Our activities with the poor are marginal."

"And overseas, many of us have become leaders in underdevelopment, that is, we are trying little projects that salve the wounds of the tortured poor while they are suffering the grossest injustices."

"The Church is part and parcel of U.S. AID programs. U.S. cornmeal goes to Caritas, and Caritas distributes it, thus holding back the tide of revolution with a few crumbs that help to keep cornmeal prices up in the United States."

"The Latin American Church, except for rare exceptions, has a hierarchy identified with the oligarchies of those lands. These oligarchies often represent less than one percent of the people. But this favorite one percent represents the greatest fans of the United States. U.S. arms strengthen their oligarchical armies and they oppress the poor even more."

"U.S. foreign policy is on a decadent course that can literally destroy this magnificent nation, and its people should not tolerate that policy."

I wrote down some scriptural and personal reflections just prior to making the decision that it was necessary to separate myself from the institutional hierarchy in order to carry out my vocation:

"Military aid is by far the majority of all aid. What a gift for hungry people."

"Good people can do horrible things in a misdirected sense of duty."

"Most priests would be better off if they had a job and earned their own keep."

"It is financial dependence and only that which keeps many of the clergy attached to the system. This financial dependence is used as a threat."

"The quality of men who filter to the top in this system are usually weak sorts, frequently they are good guys, or they can fiddle while Rome burns. They can get angry about minutia. They can strain out the gnat and swallow the camel."

"Diminishment is necessary in all human life but this is natural diminishment. It may be either psychological or physical diminishment. But people should not tolerate diminishment from an institutional source."

"The attitude of Lyndon Baines Johnson before the slaughter of Vietnam is symbolic of our time and is similar to bishops and religious superiors who seek the diminishment of their charismatic subjects."

"Catholics are hawks because they are more impregnated with the spirit of capitalism than they are with the spirit of Christ."

"Actually, our problems are not doctrinal. I am being hindered from proclaiming the word of God. For this I was ordained. While I have life I will not be silent. The word of God must be proclaimed in the real world. It cannot be proclaimed in a vacuum. It is the desire to proclaim in a vacuum that has sterilized the Church."

"The word of God is a two-edged sword but our churches have become a place to give consolation to people. Christianity is not to be a spiritual tranquilizer, it is meant to put people into life more fully. 'I have come so that they may have life and have it to the full.'" (John 10: 10)

"A catalyst is an agent outside of a chemical reaction, which causes that reaction to take place. United States' policy is causing guerrilla warfare to be an imperative necessity. The guerrilla movement of Latin America is taking on a Christian mystique."

"Someone is killing my brother. I must defend my brother. The self-definition I heard from the guerrillas was, 'I am a teacher. I am forbidden to teach in my corrupt country. Hence, I must defend myself with arms and continue teaching.'"

"The daily institutional violence is greater than armed violence. Armed violence is the lesser of two evils. The dignity of the human person violated by daily hunger is more serious than the threat of armed resistance."

The following diary entries were made during a four-day period at a Maryknoll Seminary in New York, December 25 to December 29, 1967. I was to wait at the seminary while the Superior General placed himself in a mood to listen to me. This waiting period gave me some time to reflect on revolutionary or liberation theology. Many of the themes referred to have since been systematized by Latin American theologians:

"To remain in the midst of institutional violence is to be a traitor to the people of God."

"What was looked upon as a limited people of God in Jewish history is now extended to all of the world, the Gentiles. But now the Gentiles and the majority of God's people are in bondage. They ask for liberation. They are looking for a God who frees. The know that false gods do not liberate. They are tempted to think that all gods are dead. But they are ready to accept a God that can act on their behalf."

"Jesus has not arrived for these people. All people have been redeemed, but all people have not been saved. Salvation of the whole person awaits. God desires that all people be saved (liberated) and come to a knowledge of the truth."

"But those who take up arms, how can they be Christian? Without a doubt, this is something that should not be necessary in the future. Peace is a goal of Christianity. But can self-defense be ruled out before institutionalized violence is eliminated?"

"Fine Catholic boys are fighting and dying in Vietnam, in an immoral war, destroying a land where they have no right to be. They are there with the blessing of their Catholic and Protestant chaplains and their bishops. They are there in the name of capitalism. I cannot imagine a more unfortunate cause for which to lose one's life."

"But we hear it said that Father goes overseas to bring the sacraments to the people. How can he give them the Eucharist when there is no community of faithful, of love, of mutual concern? In place of love in Latin America we have people literally buying masses and referring to themselves as the owner of the mass. People paying their church as much as one thousand dollars for a wedding. Poor people who cannot afford to be married. Hungry people who live worse than any healthy pig in the United States."

"Where is the community? Rich landowners who pay their laborers forty cents a day are given papal honors because they have given money to build a church."

"There are too many churches in Latin America and not enough Christians. Often there will be two churches at one intersection, both trying to sell masses, sell baptisms, and sell all the other products of God. This simony must be stopped."

"But how will the priests live? Many of these fine men, in place of a life that is basically parasitic to society could work at whatever they were qualified for, teachers in public schools, etc. And they could celebrate the mysteries of the Lord when the occasion called for it and not for the sake of money."

"When the Cuban government took the schools from the religious orders, many of those priests, brothers and sisters left the island. Very few were ordered to leave, but large numbers left simply because their schools were closed. They did not know how to function without their wealthy schools. Actually, they could have done much for Cuba if they had stayed."

"The conditions of Latin America are so extreme that extreme solutions are demanded. Alternatives are made nearly impossible by present U.S.-Latin American relations. U.S. intervention will escalate any wars of liberation in Latin America. The only workable Latin American defense is unity."

"It is curious that the Latin American regional superiors are now writing to the Superior General here in New York about the failure of the faculty and seminary training that results in young priests getting married within less than one year after their ordination.

"But it seems to me that the error is not in the training. The error is in the system, the error is in the failure to read the signs of the times. The error is in the inhumanity of a system that makes a law of celibacy rather than simply announcing the virtue of celibacy."

"It is strange that I find myself wanting to protect the venerable old institution, that is, I would like to see many of the fine scholars who are ready to leave stay within and reform it rather than leave it. But I suppose some will overreact. They have lived in an artificial world of study and of books and perhaps are too brittle."

"It seems to me we can avoid this schism that is to come only if the institution acknowledges its sins and errors. Currently anything will be tolerated as long as it is irrelevant."

"I am amazed at the coldness of the institution toward priests seeking laicization. Basically, they are given one day to get off the property and are offered no financial help. The Department of Water and Power has more love in its heart than such a structure."

—5—
Reflections Within the Belly of the Beast

We Need Less Data and More Values

Before we are all vaporized in a nuclear disaster, it might be in order to reflect on our values. I suppose this is why we have such phenomena as the Moral Majority. Searching for values is fundamental. I wish to express some value studies that might contrast rather boldly with the Moral Majority position. I want to look at the scriptures in the light of liberation, both personal and collective.

Taking a somewhat chronological view of the New Testament, we see the prayer of Mary, the Mother of Jesus, as she went to visit her cousin Elizabeth who was about to give birth to John the Baptist. Many theological disputants would enter upon a discussion of the virginity or the non-virginity of Mary. I believe that such reflections are diversionary wastes of time. Reams of paper have gone into such casuistry.

To me the substantive value is in the content of the words of Mary:

> He has shown the power of his arm, he has routed the proud of heart. He has pulled down princes from their thrones and exalted the lowly. The hungry he has filled with good things, the rich sent empty away. (Luke 1; 51-53)

Taking the words direct from the Mother of Jesus, we can conclude that God has a bias for the poor and that he does show might in his arm. Personally, I see the might of God's arm in the liberation struggles around the world. These struggles represent the New Exodus; the word of Moses and the example of Jesus are not out of date. So the mighty are being put down from their thrones and the lowly exalted. This is surely the work of God. The lowly are exalted by becoming the subject of society instead of the object. The fetishization of labor, that is, the consideration of people as "cheap labor," labor as a commodity, is surely the sin identified here.

77

The creative power of God is reflected in workers. To oppress workers is to oppress the power of God. We see here in these words of the Mother of Jesus the identification of oppression as *the sin* and liberation as *the virtue*. Applying this to modern economic theory, this relates to the surplus value of labor. This theory explains how workers manufacture much more wealth than they earn in salary each day. The difference between the wealth created by an individual worker and what is taken home as salary is precisely what is stolen from the worker, taken away by the owners of the means of production. This surplus value theory is applicable today. An individual worker can manufacture $5,000 worth of wealth in the course of a day and leave the factory with a $50 income. Even correcting to take account of the cost of components and wear and tear of equipment, the difference is huge.

It is the work of God to overthrow those who oppress workers. Hence, we see the mighty being put down; the Czars, the Shahs, the Ayatollahs, the Somozas, the military marionettes of El Salvador and Guatemala.

We can't say that in the history of warfare every war has been a war of liberation. But we can surely say that this is what we are seeing today in Africa, Asia, and Latin America. Of course there are excesses in these wars, even on the part of those fighting for liberation. But certainly their cause is just. And, unfortunately, if we are going to use this type of analysis we must accept the fact that the United States is not on the side of God, which is the side of the poor.

The United States, through its Central Intelligence Agency, has sent anti-Castro Cuban exiles to the National Palace of Guatemala to staff the death squads. What is the faith of the death squads? It is the faith of those who believe we can burn books and destroy an idea; it is the faith of those who believe we can kill people and stop a movement.

The position of the United States in Central America is similar to that of the Roman Empire when it issued the decree "non licet esse christianus (it is not legal to be a Christian). The death penalty was applied to the breaking of this law. Empires believe that ideas can be killed. Empire is static and stagnant. Most empires have fallen because they could not maintain troops in their distant colonies. The industrial deterioration of the United States is now costing us some 15 billion dollars a month in negative balance of payments. On top of this we have maintained a stultified troop presence in Asia, Europe and Latin America. Aside from paying our own nationals we are expending billions to pay mercenary terrorists in Nicaragua, Mozambique, Camboida, Angola, and many other places yet to be uncovered. Empire and christianity are incompatible.

Yes, we need a spiritual revitalization in the United States. It will not be brought to us by book burners, opponents of scientific research, or xenophobic preachers. It will be brought to us by understanding liberation inherent in the scriptures and the themes we can find therein. Indeed, this analysis is not meant to be sectarian any more than Jesus was sectarian. If the mode of understanding is Rabbinic, Buddhist, or Islamic, it can bear liberation interpretation. One of the great characteristics of Jesus was his ability to look to other religions, such as the Samaritans and the Syrians.

Personally, my understanding of liberation has had a biblical orientation and that is what I wish to share with you at this time. I do not believe that liberation is understood through the New Testament exclusively. But for me the New Testament has been an excellent media for understanding liberation.

Some have learned liberation through atheistic humanism and as such have formed the basis for an international vanguard of liberation. Because of my background as a priest and Christian missionary, I think that for some the New Testament will be the road to personal and collective liberation.

It is not a matter of getting one's head on straight first and then getting into the struggle. It is a matter of getting into the struggle and thereby having one's head finally straightened out. We of the middle class in the United States represent the richest one percent of the world's people.

The greatest single myth of our culture is the concept of powerlessness. We are not powerless. It is incumbent on us to demonstrate the power we have through mass mobilization and organization. The people of Nicaragua, El Salvador, and Guatemala have made it possible for us to study scripture outside of the realm of empire, outside of a controlled press which describes both sides in the conflict as "two extremes." We must be able to distinguish between the aggressor and the victim if we are to be people of discernment. It is clear to international observers of the Central American war: the United States together with the local oligarchies and their militaries represents aggression.

It is the poor people of Central America who assure us of the correct understanding of the words of the Mother of Jesus cited above.

Our culture is marked by depression. People are isolated and alienated. It is important for us to take a look at a formula for happiness and liberation. Practically all philosophers have tried to explain how to be happy. In its simplicity, I will opt for the sermon on the mount, "Happy are the poor in spirit; theirs is the kingdom of heaven." (Matthew 5; 3-13.)

I believe we can have a sense of poverty of spirit by going seven or eight thousand feet up in the mountains at night and looking at the stars. Our poverty of spirit is simply truth: we are less than a grain of sand in the universe individually. But we are something special as

connected to the whole creation. Understanding our individual poverty is the key to participation in the richness of collective struggle.

"Happy the gentle; they shall have the earth for their heritage." It
is precisely the gentle people of the earth who are capable of the sense
of outrage needed. Farm workers and urban workers who are ready
and willing to give their lives to quiet toil and who are rightfully
outraged by the denial of what is needed for a minimum subsistence,
whether in the fields of California or the fields of Central America.
Surely it will never be the crass or the cruel who will have the sensitiv-
ity to have the earth for their heritage. The greedy want it all. The
gentle will both liberate the earth and have it for their collective
possession.

"Happy those who mourn; they shall be comforted." We do not
have to mourn outside of our immediate family if we don't want to. But
it is the limitation of concerns that make us stagnant. Should we have
the good fortune to consider all children our children and the willingness to mourn with the world's suffering, we open up a vast familial
relationship with our world and we are comforted by our place in it.

"Happy are those who hunger and thirst for what is right; they
shall be satisfied." We may not be able to fight every battle. But we
had better decide just what battles we wish to fight during our short
lives. We do not have to be well adjusted to exploitation and deca-
dence. We do not have to be well adjusted to the injustices all around
us. We were built for struggle. To strive for justice is to truly live. All of
us want satisfaction. We will have as much satisfaction as we have a
functional hunger and thirst for justice.

"Happy the merciful; they shall have mercy shown to them." Life
has been reduced to a meaningless giggle by those who don't understand mercy. Nuke Iran! Nuke Russia! And I suppose we will soon
hear, Nuke France! The crazed homicide of the Manson Family was
more bearable than the glib conspiracies of modern diplomacy. It is
exactly the humanistic, idealistic, and altruistic desires for mercy and
love that are crushed out of our youth by the conventional wisdom of
our institutions. What our society calls the problem is the answer.
Humanism is not the problem, it is the solution.

"Happy are those who are pure in heart; they shall see God." And who are
the pure in heart? Integral people who do not shape their values by
opportunism. The world is full of hired guns, mercenaries who will do
anything for a price and take any side for a price. But the pure of heart
have a compass, a direction and they see God. Certainly to do justice is
to see God and to know God.

"Happy the peace makers; they shall be called children of God."
Peacemaking is never passive. Peacemaking means conflict with
what Jesus called "the world." Selfishness, greed, oppression, and
racism are a formula for eternal war. But the children of God are peace

makers, and they are infallible. These were the people who opposed
the war in Indochina, and these are the people who oppose the draft,
nuclear war, and the genocide in Central America. These are the peacemakers. They are not only children of God, they are soldiers of God.

"Happy are those who are persecuted in the cause of right; theirs
is the kingdom of heaven." Yes, there is a price for happiness; it is to
feel the hatred of the forces of evil, the forces of convention, and the
ignorance and malice of empire and its principles.

But what should we be afraid of? Nothing can preserve this tenu-
ous physical life for more than a hundred years or so. How foolish it
would be to live in a vacuum and to be dead but unburied.

"Happy are you when people abuse you and persecute you and
speak all kinds of calumny against you on my account. Rejoice and be
glad, for your reward will be great in heaven; this is how they persecuted the prophets before you." (Matthew 5; 3-13.)

I offer this formula for your happiness.

It is important to see the other side of the Moral Majority. Many
themes of the Moral Majority are a perfect description of what I would
call heresy and blasphemy. They have substituted the flag of a nation
for the word of God. They have implied that the foreign policy of the
United States expresses the teachings of Jesus.

On the contrary, the position of the scriptures is one of liberation.
The scriptures do not include hatred for the Soviets, nor glorification
of Israeli acts of terror against the Palestinians and Lebanese. The
scriptures direct us to live together on this planet as a family. Yet, I
have heard some of these electronic preachers speak of a nuclear war
as a sign of the Second Coming of Jesus. We should not and must not
allow the moral and ethical reins of the United States to be grabbed by
a group of charlatans who are apparently out for a fast buck.

We are "fortunate" to have a President who is in favor of labor
organization in Poland. Perhaps we will some day see presidential
support for labor in the United States. As you know, we do not have a
unionized country. We have a country in which less than 20 percent of
the work force is organized. Over 80 percent of our workers are non-
union. This gives us one of the lowest levels of labor organization in
the Western industrial world.

I have been trying to express how the people of Central America
become revolutionaries and how it is that Christians become revolutionaries. One of the ways this happens is by reading scripture and
acting on its values.

Here is a sermon given by Jesus for his first public address in
Nazareth:

> He came to Nazareth where he had been brought up,
> and went into the synagogue on the sabbath day as he
> usually did. He stood up to read, and they handed him the

scroll of the prophet Isaiah. Unrolling the scroll he found the place where it is written: The spirit of the Lord has been given to me. For he has annointed me, he has sent me to bring good news to the poor, to proclaim the Lord's year of favor.

He then rolled up the scroll, gave it back to the assistant and sat down. All eyes in the synagogue were fixed on him. He then began to speak to them. This text is being fulfilled today...even as you listen. And he won the approval of all, and they were astonished at the gracious words that came from his lips.

Hence, we find liberation as the very essence of the message of Jesus. We don't have to stretch it at all. He is quoting Isaiah verbatim. What is good news to the poor? Certainly it includes the right to eat, the right to study, the right to have sight, the right to have health. And this is bad news for the rich.

Jesus lost his following when he broke with sectarianism and when he broke with closed ethnic and political viewpoints. He began to speak about the works of God outside the Jewish community. He spoke of Elijah as sent to a widow of Zarephath, a Sidonian town. And he spoke of the prophet Elisha as sent to cure the Syrian leper Naaman. "No prophet is ever accepted in his own country." Whereas the synagogue accepted his initial comments about liberation, they rejected his application as he explained the work of God outside the folk community in which they lived.

When they heard this, everyone in the synagogue was enraged. They sprang to their feet and hustled him out of the town. And they took him up to the brow of the hill their town was built on...intending to throw him over the cliff, but he slipped through the crowd and walked away. (Luke 4)

It seems to me that this is the perfect response to any good sermon. A truly good sermon would lead either to opposition or to a change of heart. In contrast, middle class religion simply asks assurance of being better than someone else, assurance of eternal life, and assurance of membership. But it does not want involvement.

For Jesus, the people of God is the whole of humanity. The people of God in the sense of a visible church is only of secondary importance. The Church must be a body conscious of the one history of the world it is called to serve. But the theology of the cross must be liberated from its alienating mystifications (for example, the interpretation of the cross in terms of reconciliation, void of conflict). Jesus the man must have the integrity of his human condition. His death must not be robbed of its historical and political reality.

The current challenge is not from the non-believer but from the non-person. Transformation must be from non-person to new person. St. Paul would be proud of the Latin American theologians of liberation. Liberation is the radical removal of all causes of alienation which prevent a person from being fully developed. The biblical message of salvation provides a reference point for an interpretation of the signs of the times in terms of conflict in human history. The conquest of sin is all struggle against exploitation and alienation in a history which is fundamentally one of exploitation and alienation.

Sin is defined as everything which hinders the upward progress of human history toward full humanization. God is known in the clamor of the poor and the weak who cry for justice. Marx and St. Paul have much in common. They both agree that evil is a total structure, that sin has a unity, and that sin is structured into civilization and has gained control of the very essence of the law. But in spite of sin and its unity, the most outstanding characteristic of our time is the demand for total justice.

A look at the policies of Washington gives us a good understanding of the New Testament concept of *the world*. The world cannot see, know, give peace or hear. The world is ahistorical; everything repeats itself. The logic of the world is the logic of what used to be, but is now custom. It is the logic of those unable to discern the hour, the time, or the opportunity. The world is closed within its own circle. It is opposed to everything new and it is essentially conservative. Everything is already fixed. It might even call itself a moral majority.

Hence, we have to avoid false interpretations which present the ministry of Jesus in individualistic, internal, apocalyptic, and apolitical terms. Certainly, Jesus was guilty according to a justice which the powerful administer in their own interests. As such, he had to die.

In our own hour, we can look at our Secretary of State making accusations regarding the Soviets' use of chemical and biological warfare. Personally, I don't have much respect for someone who criticizes the behavior of others and is doing things that are as bad. This is called hypocrisy and this is the thing that led to the outrage of Jesus time and time again in the scriptures. It would be interesting to mark the percentage of time in the New Testament that Jesus is in a state of rage over this type of hypocrisy. Before we begin to castigate the Soviets for allegations we cannot even prove, let us look to our own armed forces. White phosphorus is now being used as a weapon to burn the non-combatants in El Salvador and Guatemala. White phosphorus clings to the skin and burns and burns until death. I asked medical personnel what can be done for someone struck by white phosphorus; immerse the entire body in water was the recommendation. This, of course, is not always possible. Our administration must respond to the white phosphorus reality. I would also like to know its role in causing denge fever in Nicaragua and Cuba. Indeed, one wonders whether biological warfare was the source of hemorrhagic conjunctivitis, tobacco blight, and pig fever in Cuba.

We have studied some of these current realities in the light of the fourth chapter of St. Luke where we hear Jesus speak of his mission to bring good news to the poor and liberty to captives. We are not able to hear the good news in the above mentioned criminality. And what about liberty to captives? We live in a highly incarcerated society here in the United States. We live in one of the most highly incarcerated lands in the world. Only the Soviet Union and the Union of South Africa have a higher percentage of their people in prison than the United States. But in terms of children in prison, the United States is number one. Aside from the children in prison (from eleven to seventeen years of age), we have over one million children who have run away. There are over 20,000 children who have simply disappeared. In addition there are tens of thousands of children working as prostitutes. Liberty to captives indeed! To set the downtrodden free, that is what Jesus said. So what of our children?

Similarly, we hear no good news from people who are interested in building 16th-century-style prisons in the U.S. I had the opportunity to speak to a presiding judge about the number of people in prison who are a danger to public safety. The judge responded that he thought about 5 percent of those locked up were such a danger. That 5 percent, therefore, represents the number of people who should be locked up. Others who have committed some crime could be in a much more creative setting such as we have seen in some European countries where people can be placed under house arrest when they are not a danger to public safety. They are permitted to go to work and to go home but they are not free to do other things until they have served their term of house arrest. Hence, they can earn money, be together with their families, and conform to the law.

By looking at the scripture in the light of liberation we are seeing a demythologized view of how to follow this teaching, how Jesus' teaching is very non-sectarian, how it is oriented toward conduct and the collectivity of people. It is not simply an individual-God-and-myself type of thing. By looking at the scriptures in this fashion we will understand the people of Central America better as they proceed toward victory in their struggles in El Salvador and Guatemala.

In chapter three of St. Luke we meet the powerful personality of St. John the Baptist.

> In the fifteenth year of Tiberius Caesar's reign, when Pontius Pilate was governor of Judaea, Herod tetrarch of Galilee, his brother Philip tetrarch of the lands of Ituraea and Trachonitis, Lysanias Annas and Caiaphas, the word of God came to John son of Zechariah, in the wilderness. He

went through the whole of Jordan district proclaiming a baptism of repentance for the forgiveness of sins, as it is written in the book of sayings of the prophet Isaiah:

A voice cries in the wilderness: "Prepare a way for the Lord, make his paths straight. Every valley will be filled in, every mountain and hill be laid low, winding ways will be straightened and rough roads made smooth. And all mankind shall see the salvation of God."

He said, therefore, to the crowds who came to be baptized by him, "Broods of vipers, who warned you to fly from the retribution that is coming? But if you are repentant, produce the appropriate fruits, and do not think of telling yourselves, 'We have Abraham for our father' because, I tell you, God can raise children for Abraham from these stones. Yes, even now the axe is laid to the roots of the trees, so that any tree which fails to produce good fruit will be cut down and thrown into the fire."

When all the people asked him, "What must we do then?" He answered, "If any has two tunics he must share with the man who has none, and the one with something to eat must do the same." (Luke 3; 1-12.)

It is significant that after this strong and mystical passage, John the Baptist proclaims the praxis, "Share." Sharing is fundamental to preparing a way for the Lord. This matter of sharing is so critical that it remains the key issue in the world today. The question of distribution of goods and services is a matter of sharing. How these things are shared and who gets what and why is a matter of politics.

So we confront the message of this rugged survivalist who lived on locusts and wild honey. As most of the prophets and the Messiah himself, John the Baptist would have been thrown out of the vast majority of today's churches. His language was too strong, he was not properly dressed. He called people snakes.

The importance of John's ministry is stressed by its exact location in time. And today, the message of John the Baptist is the answer to our international crisis. "Share."

At this time in Iran we can observe one sector of the population being crucified. As many as 150 of the Mujahadeen are being executed every day. There is no sharing, just slaughter. I cannot speak as an expert on Iranian politics. I have never been to Iran. But my very distance from the subject might be an opportunity to apply certain theoretical political positions.

I cannot take a sectarian position either politically or religiously. I believe that sectarianism is the center of the Iranian crisis. But I can and do take the position that it is time for progressive Americans to examine the Iranian reality and to support the people of Iran as they restructure their society.

The people of Iran obviously sought a personification of their cultural integrity as they organized against the tyranny of the Shah. The symbol and person of this unity was the Ayatollah Khomeini. His amazing return to Iran and the exodus of the Shah will be remembered as the definitive end of the monarchy, and the beginning of popular government. People of good will from all over the world supported this new direction in Iran and rejoiced to see exiles return from all over the world. But since the euphoria of 1979, each day has dampened the spirit of progressive Iranians.

It does not seem possible to built a functional polity based on a theocratic structure. This has been a common problem in the Middle East. Closed ethnic politics always become reactionary politics. The lesson of history is clear. There will never be a Jewish state that is successfully exclusive of other ethnic groups. There will never be an Arab state where democracy flourishes unless it is a secular state.

I must condition my remarks by acknowledging that cultural, historical, and traditional national characteristics will certainly mark the personality of any new polity. But religion itself cannot be the decisive element. Just look at the world's religions. In each case we have the spectrum from reactionary to revolutionary. There are revolutionary Buddhists of the Sangha and reactionary Buddhists who call them devils. There are progressive Jews who abhor the policies of the Israeli government and who object to the vicious treatment of their Arab brothers and sisters, and there are reactionary Jews. There are Catholic priests who are agents of the CIA and there are Catholic priests and nuns who are revolutionary leaders. There are Mullahs like the Ayatollah Talegani who understand political pluralism and there are reactionary Mullahs who would kill anyone disagreeing with their ignorant ideas. It is clear that religious sects are not the issue. It is clear that the religious membership of citizens is irrelevant. What is relevant is both the conduct of citizens and the conduct of government.

Political history tells us that the only future with any stability in Iran will be a structure which includes respect for all of the people—the Kurds, the Baluchis, the Turkomans, and Arabs, the Jews, the Christians and the atheists. The religious tag of the citizens is not relevant. The willingness of the citizens to comply with the common good is relevant. I do not believe we have to discuss the end of the reign of the Ayatollah Khomeini. Nature will take care of that. But we do need a methodology of unification, an instrument for coalescing the progressive forces regardless of their religious or ethnic background.

A people's government must be one in which there is no political disease. By dis-ease I mean that no one should be uncomfortable because of their ethnic or religious background. To have ethnic groups who are considered outsiders is to find the formula for perpetual war. This formula does not have a future.

I believe there is a Central America analogy to the Iranian situation. When the Romero dictatorship was overthrown in El Salvador in 1979, many progressive Salvadorans from the academic and political communities aligned themselves with the new military-civilian junta. When these people tried to assert themselves on behalf of the people, they were confronted with raw military power, in the form of escalating torture and murder of Salvadoran citizens. As a matter of integrity, all progressive forces left the junta. An example of this is Guillermo Ungo, who initially served on the junta and who is now president of the Democratic Revolutionary Front (FDR).

In a similar fashion we have daily reports of people of integrity in Iran who are bound to separate themselves from the governmental slaughter taking place in their country. They do not support the executions, they do not support the lack of civil rights, and they are organizing from within to change things. Others are active in international exile and solidarity work. The assurance with which people view the failure of the current polity of Iran has led to the formation of the National Council of Resistance, a concept so democratic that it could be legalized in any progressive nation.

The art of revolution is the art of uniting forces. If all of the political organizations still within Iran are written off as the enemy, a great error will have been made. On the contrary, all elements within the country, both religious and secular, must be attracted by the logic of the new council. Consider some of the points of the National Council of Resistance: guarantees of complete freedom of expression, political and religious belief and opinion; freedom of the media; legitimization of the rights of the regional people across the country, particularly the right of the Kurdish people to determine their own affairs; guarantee of political, social, and economic equality between men and women in every sphere of life; support for all revolutionary, anti-dictatorial, anti-colonialist and anti-exploitation movements around the world. Iranians have the right to build such a future.

I am not in the business of selecting candidates or representatives for the Iranian people. But I have here some comments of the former president, Bani Sadr:

> It is not like the time of the Shah, it's even worse. Most of the Savak agents were rehired; 80 percent of old Savak agents work for Khomeini's new secret police. The same files are still there. The same methods are there. Before there were at least certain formalities, now there's nothing, just simple killing!

And what is the best way to unify a people? Start a war. Reagan seems to understand the principle. Could the war with Iraq be a matter of trying to gain support for the Iranian military? Then as the left and the mullahs kill each other off, the military will assume power; they might even enthrone a king. This is not a certainty, it is a question.

As a distant observer, it seems to be that the above scenario can be avoided by the formation of a National Council of Resistance. Now is the time to invite all progressive elements in Iran to participate. This is not a time for denouncing those who have stayed within the current government. If all sectors are invited into the National Council of Resistance, it will certainly succeed.

True revolutionaries are driven by deep feelings of love. Class conflict does not mean personal hatred. I am sure the Iranian people do not intend to allow the fanatics, the hypocrites, and the ignoramuses to govern. We need more universities in Iran, not less. We need more schools, not less. We need less religious fanaticism, not more.

We have an analogous group in the United States calling itself the Moral Majority. They have little knowledge of Jesus or of politics. But they have decided to make the foreign policy of the United States their religion. I don't think our people are going to take that and I don't think the Iranians are going to take it either.

The National Council of Resistance does not have all of the answers. The answers will flow as people are empowered to make decisions. Those who think they have all the answers are the fanatics, the dogmatists, the closed sectarians, and the racists. We have to speak with humble sincerity. The coalition must include everyone. It is a matter of winning hearts, speaking as people with faith in God and faith that the revolution is in progress. The old language must be put aside, the old methods must be forgotten. We cannot speak of stupid executions in the future. We cannot talk of torture. These are the tools of people who are already defeated.

Every execution plants the seeds of resistance. Every act of torture does the same. There must be a society built without executions, without filthy prisons, and without torture. Those incapable of such humanity do not deserve to govern. Any government using torture should not exist. In Iran today, the Mujahadeen, the liberation theologians and liberation activists of Iran, are being mercilessly executed. This must stop. To be viable, society must exist for the people, not for those who are in high places.

War on the U.S. Poor

The great prophet John the Baptist instructed us:

> If anyone has two tunics he must share with the man who has none, and the one with something to eat must do the same.

If this applies on the micro scale, it certainly must apply on the macro scale. In responding affirmatively to John's directive we have the answer to world hunger.

A government for the people would foster production for the people. But the current productive apparatus of the United States is in direct opposition to the needs of the people of the United States. It's all there in the Reagan budget. Translating the mystical figures, I read: increased mental and physical disease; decreased worker productivity; increased crime; a decrease in learning capability together with hunger and malnutrition in the world's wealthiest nation.

The brunt of this economic disaster will be borne by infants, children, the elderly, the disabled, the working poor and single parents, mainly women. After all, what political debts does the president owe to those people? Over one million people have been removed from the food stamp rolls. Millions of students are paying higher prices for their subsidized lunches, or have been dropped from the lunch program. The Women-Infant-Children (WIC) program, providing milk, cereals and juices for pregnant women, infants, and children under five, is under constant assault from administration budget cutters. The Social Security Program, which is funded by a second federal income tax on working citizens, will simply be allowed to fail to deliver what was promised. Patient fees for Medicare have been increased. Government assistance for housing has been decimated. CETA has been wiped out. Many other programs serving poor and working people are feeling the budget ax.

The con men and sales pitch experts in Washington talk about budget cutting. But they have not uncovered the third shell. There is actually no budget cutting at all. There is only the most reckless program of spending in the history of the U.S. They neglect to mention that nearly two trillion dollars in military spending over five years is unrelated to the security of the country. On the contrary, it places all of us in peril. The largest entrepreneur in the U.S., the Pentagon, has now taken power in a quiet move tantamount to a military coup.

The United States started the cold war at Hiroshima and confirmed it at Nagasaki. The Soviet Union accepted the challenge and made it clear that they did not lose twenty million citizens defeating Adolph Hitler to give in to U.S. dominance. Each point of cold war escalation by the U.S. was followed by the USSR some five to ten years later. What began with a U.S. nuclear war against Japan must be terminated by U.S. initiative. With their criminal plotting and planning to murder 200 million non-combatants in a first strike massacre, the homicidal maniacs and reckless throw-away spenders in the Pentagon are the cause of both inflation and unemployment.

There is nothing complicated about it. Economists, like lawyers are hired to make things complex. The reality is simple. You just cannot manufacture hundreds of billions of dollars in totally useless items, you cannot pay hundreds of billions in salaries to completely non-productive people, and not expect the value of each useful item to soar. Too many dollars are looking for too few useful items. A five thousand dollar house now draws one hundred thousand dollars because of military induced inflation. Millions are jobless because of the tiny number of people hired per million dollars spent in military production.

Rather than deal with reality, the extremists now in power are trying to prove that our economic crisis is related to the government serving the needs of people in health and social services. There is no such connection. The U.S. has very low per capita expenditures for health and social services compared with the rest of the industrial world.

Some of the pop economics coming from Washington seems to imply that money is a constant. But the place of money is historically relative. As we slowly demythologize we may understand that any relationship between money and health care is a clear sign of an underdeveloped economy. In a truly developed society there will be no relationship between health care and money. In an underdeveloped society there is a relationship between education and money. A developed society will remove that barrier. Similarly, lowering the importance of money in society will immediately lower the level of crime.

At the present time there is one aspect of the U.S. economy which is truly socialized and that is our cost. Each and every one of us shares in paying the cost of each item we buy. We find this out when we buy a hamburger or pay the rent. We all pay together. But the sick joke in all of this is that while cost is socialized, profits are privatized. We can't perpetuate the myth that poverty and wealth are unrelated. As we become conscious we will understand that wealth is the cause of poverty.

Just as wealth is related to poverty so are development and underdevelopment related internationally. Underdeveloped countries were not poor in their native state. Their underdevelopment is created and is directly related to what is called development. Such development includes taking raw materials and commodities from poor nations and appropriating accrued profits by foreign interests.

We just can't go on maintaining the myth of a free world that is capitalistic and a slave world that is socialistic. Such a scenario implies that the dictatorships of Chile, Philippines, Paraguay, Guatemala, El Salvador, Haiti, South Korea, Taiwan, and many others are somehow in the "free world." Clearly what distinguishes "free world" from "slave world" for government propagandists is whether a country allows U.S. corporations to export its wealth, or at least has a chance to do so.

Patriots in the Streets

In recent decades there has been a continuous voice of truth in the United States. It has not been the government. It has been the patriots in the streets. Those who demonstrated for peace and civil rights in the sixties and seventies were clearly vindicated by history. Administrations of the 60s and 70s are under a cloud. The people were right in their opposition to the Indochina War. The people were right in demanding civil rights legislation. And the people opposing militarism today are equally right. Patriots opposing intervention in El Salvador, Guatemala, Nicaragua, and Honduras are right. Government functionaries supporting the interventionist position of the United States have shown no "expertise." Why not get on the right side for once? Why not support the struggles for liberation? This is the only way we can free ourselves from a nonsensical foreign policy. We have only dictators and fascists as friends. With an intelligent and internationalist approach we could share in the global integration of a just and functional economy.

Once conscious of reality, we can understand that production determines consumption. Military production creates wars. We will use our weapons. We always have.

The power of production determining consumption is obvious in the world of ideas, music, television, movies, Twinkies, and Coke. We "eat" these items not because of inherent value but simply because they are produced and advertised. They are what is available and known. We make ourselves like what is available and known, or else we go hungry.

The notion that our economy will operate without planning is indeed an odd one. The Reagan administration is operating on an old book, *The Wealth of Nations* by Adam Smith, published in 1776. Smith believed the economy would be regulated by an "invisible hand." Upon questioning, one would find that Smith believed that hand was the hand of God.

Contrary to the beliefs of Smith and the White House, the only kind of production worthwhile is that which is based on the needs of people. We need low-cost housing, we need public transportation, quality education, and health care for all. We will never have these necessities under a Reagan administration. We will never have these necessities for all under a market system that prioritizes profit for the few.

Selfishness as a necessity permeates our environment. The natural communal feelings of children are successfully crushed by our school systems. They are taught to get smart and to realize that "business is business" and that "this is not a charitable institution." We are teaching them the problem. The solution is to free up their natural selflessness, their natural humanism, their natural desire to view society in a familial manner.

It is sad to see how many opportunist pharisees have made a religion out of Washington's policies. They are even trying to tell us that Christianity is not humanistic. If it's not humanistic, it's not Christianity.

Probably the greatest single myth on our current political environment is that we are helpless. We are not helpless. We are powerful. We have to get this government off our backs. It's not delivering for the people. It is delivering for the corporations. We simply do not have the functional political entity needed at this time. The Democratic Party is not the party of labor; it is the party of corporate capital. Hence, we have two parties of corporate capital.

We need the political power of people who work. Pope John Paul II made that clear in his democratically socialistic encyclical, *Laborem Exercens*. Labor can be managerial, intellectual, professional, skilled or unskilled. Such work power would be worthy of the wonderful people of the United States.

In order to have the kind of political apparatus needed, we have to grow in political consciousness. After years of misinformation, I suppose most people probably believe that the rich support the poor. Don't we hear it all the time? "We're tired of supporting *those* people." "We're tired of paying the bill for those people." In reality, the poor support the rich. The poor do the work. And the more distasteful and dangerous the work, the less they are paid. The poor plant, pick, cook, and serve our food, and bus the dishes. The poor make the country function. The reality is that the rich don't have to work at all. If they have something in the bank, they get money for doing nothing. Whether their money came from organized crime, dope or prostitution, if it is in the bank they do not have to work at all to receive income.

On the other hand, those who don't have money must pay to get it. Try to borrow a hundred dollars sometime. You will pay up to a hundred and fifty dollars for it. It is not acceptable to see our public servants living like royalty and telling the peasants to tighten their belts...to eat jelly beans. Inflation means that the poor suffer more. The affluent are reimbursed with higher interest on their money.

Unfortunately, the labor movement in the United States was domesticated by business unionism. Collective bargaining was confined to wages and fringe benefits. As a result there is no party of labor and no attempt on the part of organized labor to control the means of production. Certainly the people working in factories can manage those factories. People pumping gas at the local service station are better prepared to serve as representatives than what we see in the Congress today. I don't believe people who work at the gas pumps would knuckle under quite as easily as Congress. I would be happy to see the transition. There is no turn to the right in the United States.

There's only a manipulation to the right by people who have been purchased.

The Reagan budget gives us an opportunity to meditate on the class nature of our society. Our poor will continue to pay money they do not have to borrow money they cannot get.

And our prisons are waiting for the poor. The majority of people incarcerated in the U.S. at this moment are technically innocent. They are waiting trial because they do not have bail money. Yes, they are incarcerated because they lack money. A tap on the wrist awaits most of the affluent should they transgress.

As I watch our local medical facilities close, as I look at the shambles of the Social Security System I have paid into for almost forty years, what shatters me is the superabundance of funds for genocide in El Salvador and Guatemala. We have plenty of money to pay for the rape and murder of nuns, the gunning down of priests, and the massacre of children.

What we have in the new "budget" is not simply tyranny, not simply taxation without representation, not simply the bankruptcy of the people of the United States and the military takeover of the economy; it is a declaration of war on the poor of the United States and a simultaneous declaration of war on the people of Central America. As an ordained exorcist, I consider this economic program to be diabolical.

Hence, the conclusion of this meditation is to accept the words of Jesus:

> "This is the kind [of devil]," he answered, "that can only be
> driven out by prayer and fasting." (Mark 9; 29)

With this in mind, I recommend a period of prayer and fasting as long as United States intervention continues in Central America; as long as we have a Reagan budget and a Pentagon government. Together with this spiritual preparation, we must add our effective organizing for resistance and victory.

Following is the Testimony of Nicaragua's Foreign Minister Miguel D'Escoto, upon initiating on Sunday night, July 7, 1985, his "Fast for Peace, for the Defense of Life Against Terrorism."

Father D'Escoto expressly stated that this Fast for Peace was undertaken as a personal expression of Christian faith and not in his official capacity as Foreign Minister of the Republic of Nicaragua.

"After a long process of prayer and discernment with the Superior of my congregation, with my Bishop, with priests, religious laity, I have decided to accept Christ's call to begin a Fast "for peace, in defense of life and against terrorism," as a prophetic prayer to put an end to the policy of state terrorism of the Government of the United States against Nicaragua so that our people will be able to live in peace and dedicate their energies to national development.

"I make this fast:

"1. So that the right to life and self-determination of the people of Nicaragua and of the peoples of Central America, of Latin America and of the world will be respected.

"2. As an expression of Christian rejection of the policy of state terrorism imposed by the U.S. Government against Nicaragua and as a religious expression of condemnation of the systematic kidnappings, torture, and assasination of our sisters and brothers by counterrevolutionaries whom the United States finances and directs.

"3. As a way of expressing my love of God, of my people, of the Church and my fervent desire that there be an end to the aggression and the beginning of a new phase in the relationship between the United States and Nicaragua that will be just and respectful of our rights as a sovereign and independent nation.

"4. To reach out in friendship to the people of the United States, cordially inviting all North Americans of good will to accompany me in this act of denunciation so that together we can achieve a just and lasting peace. I extend my hand and my voice to the oppressed people of Latin America so that they may reinforce with their prayer and action the aspirations of justice of the Nicaraguan people.

"5. As a way of unmasking those who abusively have proclaimed themselves defenders of the most sacred Judeo-Christian values with which they try to justify their own immoral and cruel war against Nicaragua.

"6. To ask pardon, the grace of repentance and change of heart of those brothers and sisters in the faith, who should have denounced the crimes being committed against our innocent people but have, instead, kept a complicity in silence with those who, following the example of Herod have ordered the massacre of our chidren, women, aged and youth.

"7. As a testimony that our people and Government harbor only the most sincere sentiments of Central American solidarity without the slightest desire to intervene in affairs that are solely within the competence of the other peoples of Central America, I ask the Lord to help change the hearts of rulers who have mistakenly allowed the use of their territories as a base of aggression against our people, involving themselves in a war by proxy which in no way can benefit their own peoples and that represents a risk of incalculable consequences for the region.

"As a Nicaraguan and from my innermost being as a priest, I make this Fast and Prayer to accompany my people in the pain which they suffer as a consequence of the aggression, and to accompany our herioc combatants who risk their lives in defense of the country. I make this fast for all my sisters and brothers who carry the cross which has been placed on them by those who attempt to deny us the right to life.

"I pray for Daniel, our President, and for all the leaders of our Revolution so that the Lord will always enlighten their path and that they remain steadfast, as they always have, at the side of the most humble and needy, in defense of justice and national sovereignty.

"I invite our Holy Father, our Bishops, and the religious leaders of Nicaragua and the world to accompany us in this act of prophetic prayer. I firmly believe that, given the aggression, we must maintain and intensify our efforts in the areas of military defense and security, in the diplomatic, economic and productive areas, as well as in the legal area, in which we have to continue struggling so that our rights as a free and sovereign nation be respected, conscious that we as Christians, besides supporting these efforts, have something very much our own to contribute in the defense of our nation. In the name of Christ, our Lord, as a Christian and as a priest, I call upon my sisters and brothers in the faith so that this Fast and Prayer will ignite in all of Nicaragua an evangelical insurrection with means of struggle which emanate from the gospel and which it is indispensable to begin to use for the coming of the reign. I ask God to increase the number of those North Americans who have pledged to resist and stop the plans of aggression of their Government and to renew the energies of all those in the world who struggle for justice, peace and against terrorism.

"I will continue in prayer and fasting until this evangelical insurrection is ignited in Nicaragua and until this spark is multiplied in actions of solidarity by women and men of good will in North America, Latin America, Europe and the third world."

—6—
Looking Down There
From Up Here

El Salvador has become a slaughterhouse. The personification of that slaughterhouse is Quality Meats, the actual name of a slaughterhouse in El Salvador used for decapitation of people. Both the Mexican and U.S. press reported on this unspeakable atrocity in 1982-83. "Some kind of expertise had to be used in this," said a Salvadoran doctor. The bodies and heads were all dumped alongside the roads in various locales, making identification difficult. Only five people were positively identified while thirty-three heads and over a hundred bodies were found. The slaughter was traced to the Quality Meats slaughterhouse located in the town of Ateos in the department of La Libertad. The workers there wrote to the Human Rights Commission of El Salvador saying that their slaughterhouse was being used for executions each night.

Alberto Pipino, an Argentine journalist working for the Mexican paper *Uno Mas Uno*, visited Quality Meats with another foreign reporter in March, 1982. They learned that the manager for Quality Meats from 1977-1979 was Hans Christ, and that his brother-in-law, Ricardo Sol-Meza, was a major stockholder in the company. Hans Christ was released on bail from a Miami jail while awaiting possible extradition to El Salvador, where he had been indicted along with Sol-Meza in the murder of two U.S. land reform advisors and the head of the Salvadoran Agrarian Reform Institute at the Sheraton Hotel in San Salvador. Salvadoran authorities have reportedly dropped charges against Sol-Meza.

Jesus said, "You shall know the truth and the truth shall make you free."

We have to see the complicity of our own government in all of this. A former CIA Director, now Vice President of the United States, had the audacity to visit the Dominican Republic, which has been so tormented by the CIA. It was not enough that he visited the country that was victimized, violated, and invaded by 40,000 U.S. troops in April 1965. The Dominican people responded to Bush's visit with demonstrations and a university boycott, expressing general public

97

outrage. Yet Bush had the gall to stand on Dominican soil and urge the people of Nicaragua to overthrow their government. Fifty thousand Nicaraguans died to end the tyranny of Anastasio Somoza and Vice President Bush would ask the Nicaraguans in their newly won victory to overthrow their government. This is like the King of England asking the people of the United States to overthrow George Washington and Thomas Jefferson.

This must be the lowest period in the history of the United States. But just as an alcoholic must hit bottom, I think we have hit bottom with the performance of George Bush.

I would like to review how El Salvador has been covered in recent years by the press and to identify the lies that have been perpetrated on the people of the United States. The first myth is the presumption that in El Salvador and Guatemala the fighting is taking place between the extreme right and the extreme left. Wrong! The U.S. press continues to talk of centrist governments looking on in dismay while extremists battle each other. That assessment is incorrect. They are unaware, as is the rest of the world, that Amnesty International has identified Guatemala and El Salvador as two of the most repressive governments on earth.

The extreme right is portrayed as a collection of isolated, fanatical groups operating on their own impetus. In reality these groups are working in close communion with both the regular military forces and the business community. The point is that the so-called extreme right, the government, and the armed forces are a unit both in El Salvador and in Guatemala.

These governments have made no attempt to stop torture, the pillaging of peasant communities, rape, or summary execution. Why? Because these vile acts are part of the governmental program in both El Salvador and in Guatemala.

The victims of this government-inspired terror are primarily unarmed villagers, not the "extreme left." Through a crafty division of labor, these governments are systematically destroying village after village of their own citizens. Why? To terrorize whole populations into accepting the poverty and degradation that is necessarily their's so long as their society's economies and polities are organized to benefit the rich landowners and corporate executives, at home and abroad in the U.S.

In El Salvador the centrists are represented by hundreds of organizations making up the Democratic Revolutionary Front (FDR). This broad based and pluralistic organization represents the majority of the people of El Salvador.

In Guatemala political and military unity is maintained through the URNG or Guatemalan National Revolutionary Union. In contrast to the FDR in El Salvador the URNG does not have a political organization outside of the country.

Myth two: Both sides use terror indiscriminantly. False. Terror is the systematic strategy of these governments. Self-defensive actions by resistance forces cannot reasonably be called terror. All of us should be able to distinguish the aggressive action of the rapist from the defensive action of the rape victim.

The Catholic Church of El Salvador documented over 12,000 murders in one year, 1980, in that country. A comparable rate in the U.S. would be 528,000 murders. There was not a single indictment. The vast majority of these people were dragged from their homes, thrown into detention centers, tortured, and murdered by the government of El Salvador.

In Guatemala over one million Indians have been displaced by government violence. As America's Watch reported in its 1984 *Guatemala: A Nation of Prisoners,* tens of thousands were and are being murdered including, as of 1984, 311 peasant leaders; 110 trade union leaders; 18 journalists; 89 university professors; 226 elementary school teachers; 389 high school and university students; 12 priests and 99 catechists; 189 people slaughtered just in Las Lomas, and this figure continues to increase as more bodies are found in clandestine cemeteries; the bombing of the towns of San Jacinto, Chimaltenango and Nebaj; the massacre of 80 peasants in Barrillas and the general military occupation of the western indigenous highlands.[1]

There is also the complicity of the Guatemalan military with that of Honduras in killing refugees from El Salvador. And now the United States is renewing military assistance to Guatemala. It is not possible that the United States is unaware of the criminal elements it is sustaining. Researchers have found a direct relationship between the presence of torture and the presence of U.S. AID in third world countries. Central America is no exception.

The killing supported by U.S. tax dollars in these countries includes the rape and murder of U.S. nuns as well as the regular use of decapitation; cutting off of hands, legs, genitals; disfiguring; and general butchery. It is intentional terror designed to frighten citizens into submission. But, it has backfired. Each such government atrocity increases the resistance because many people have seen their relatives executed for joining labor unions, joining student organizations, participating in peasant leagues or even accepting leadership in religious study groups.

Myth Three: The question of Central America is one of ideology. Wrong again! It is not a matter of dogma. It is a question of human need. You can't have a tiny country like El Salvador covered with coffee trees and expect to have a well-nourished people. Although the coffee bean has no food value, it does produce cash and that cash is shared by 2 percent of the people. We in the U.S. have instant coffee. They, in Central America, have starvation. Instant coffee, of course, has profits.

The right to live life fully, or even at all, is not currently enjoyed in Central America. The legacy of the United States in Guatemala and El Salvador is misery, ignorance, and disease. Nicaragua has done more for its people in six years than was accomplished in its entire history of dependency to Spain, England, and the U.S. And they have done it while under threat of annihilation.

Myth four: Those who oppose the land reform program in El Salvador have no desire for peace. Not so. The masses of the Salvadoran people understood the motives of the land reform program from the very beginning. It was merely a covert plan to exterminate the organizations of resistance. It was a program of rural pacification. Central American missionaries gathered in Mexico City to discuss their plight made the following statement on the land reform program in November of 1980:

> We condemn the program in Central America of The American Institute of Free Labor Development, the joint creation of the AFL-CIO and United States big business. This nefarious organization, long a front for CIA activities in the hemisphere has participated in the design and execution of the distorted "land reform of the Salvadoran Military Junta." This program is an exact repetition of the Phoenix Program of the Vietnam War and is even under the same Director. It gives the use of a small piece of land to those who cooperate blindly with the regime and openly slaughter opponents.[2]

Indeed, less than one percent of the coffee lands are affected by these so called reforms. None of the land is being turned over to campesinos as personal property. A monthly fee is required for use of the land. Whenever it pleases the government can merely raise the rent and thereby evict all campesinos. In fact, the principal recipients of land in El Salvador have been members of ORDEN, the largest "private" security force in El Salvador, at 30,000 strong.

Myth five: The situation in Central America is very complex, you can't tell the good guys from the bad guys. Yes you can. It's easy. The good guys are not pleased that 2 percent of the people own over 60 percent of the land. The good guys object to the fact that 30 percent of the people subsist on a per capita income of five dollars a month and another 58 percent have a per capita income of only ten dollars a month. The good guys are offended because more than 40 percent of the urban sector and over 60 percent of the rural sector are illiterate in Central America. They do not accept the fact that half of the children must die before the age of five.

The good guys know that all of this is due to gross oppression by the bad guys, who have the wealth and flaunt it. The good guys are the ones who rebel against injustice.

One final myth: The United States is trying to help improve things. Believing this is like believing we destroyed the villages to save them in Vietnam. Certainly the presence of the U.S. is no help to the people of Central America. The only reason the U.S. is intervening directly in Central America is because the people there are winning. Why would U.S. troops be there if the oligarchies could fight their own battles? The oligarchies are losing and once again the U.S. aligns with the losers, the oppressors. Perhaps, as in Vietnam, our presence will cause so much dislocation, so much pain, so much death and destruction of people and infrastructure that even when the people win there will be little left for them. If so, it will not be an accident. It will be policy. If the U.S. government cannot prevent people from overthrowing oligarchies it is intent, at a minimum, in insuring that the new emerging societies will be so poor and so crippled by the legacy of pain they have suffered that they will not provide models of a better life for others to emulate. Regrettably, in fact, we destroy the villages to destroy them.

Simultaneously, war is being declared on the poor of the United States by an extremist administration that wipes out thousands of CETA jobs and replaces them with nothing, that removes people from food stamps and replaces the program with nothing, that is cutting back on social security benefits upon which the elderly depend, and that does all of this in the name of budget cutting, while creating the most reckless military spending spree in the history of the United States. Indeed, while the U.S. steals the tax money from the poor of the U.S., it is simultaneously using that money to kill the poor of Central America. Personally, I don't think people in the U.S. are going to tolerate such tyranny forever, and I congratulate the people of Central America for the victorious position they have taken.

I would like to share some ideas that I believe to be true and which I believe will make us all free.

I believe a new international economic order is essential for world peace. I believe the current economic order has no prospect of ending misery in the United States or anywhere else. I believe that production based solely on motives of corporate profit will simply lead to more and more poverty.

I believe that the nation state as the terminus of sovereignty is as outdated as the city states of past centuries. I believe that the goals of

the United Nations are substantive and that the member states of the
United Nations have more in common today than did our thirteen
colonies prior to our coming together as a nation.

I believe that we cannot have a functional economy in the United
States and maintain a half million troops in Europe for thirty-five
years or thousands of troops in Korea for thirty years, or anywhere
else, for that matter.

What is needed today is bilateralism and that is what the nations
of the Third World are looking for after years of unilateral proclama-
tions from the so-called developed world. The conditions of bilateralism include a principal focus on the urgent needs of the people in poor
countries.

I believe it is sinful for any nation to export food while its own
people go hungry. We find many nations exporting food not only for
people in other lands, but for cattle, while their own people don't eat. It
is estimated that if cattle in the United States were fed grass instead of
grain the loss here would merely be that our steaks would be somewhat less tender. The profits of agribusiness companies would probably suffer somewhat. Meanwhile, if properly distributed, the surplus
grain would be sufficient to end starvation throughout the entire
world. This reminds me of a similarly sad state of affairs which
prevailed many years ago when soda pop manufacturers were storing
up quinine and people were dying of malaria for want of it. Is this sort
of thing murder without the smoking gun? It is certainly death for no
good reason. Death by preventable and curable diseases, death by
starvation and oligarchic policy is unnecessary and thus criminal.

What would be involved in a New International Economic Order?
Certainly one of the issues is regional planning, that is, to concentrate
on the basic needs of the region rather than to simply consider what
foreign corporate capital desires for the region. The two perspectives
have nothing in common. Next comes integration. That is the formation of common currencies and common banking systems on a
regional basis. Economic integration will lead to political integration;
instead of having many separate island states in the Caribbean, I
believe we need to have a Caribbean Federation with a common
currency and a regional economy. I believe that Central America will
be a single nation in the future, including Belize and Panama. A
region would be made of the Andean states, another of the nations of
the Southern Cone, and Brazil would stand on its own.

The new international economic order will not be based on supply-
side nonsense. It was supply-side economics that gave us the crash of
1929. We had produced so many supply items which few could buy that
the economy stopped and died, and the economy will crash again

unless there is a conversion in the minds of those running the economics of our country.

By looking at some of these issues and thinking about them, we will understand the poor nations better. The truth will make us free and will at the same time liberate them from their misery. Yes, each nation must give up some of its sovereignty in order to have a functional international political order.

Negotiations, not war, is a key ingredient of just international political order. Nicaraguan President Daniel Ortega Saavedra was authorized to present a peace proposal on behalf of the Salvadoran FDR at the thirty sixth session of the U.N. General Assembly:

> If today our people are waging an armed struggle under the leadership of its organizations, the FMLN and the FDR, this is because oppressive and repressive regimes have closed all peaceful avenues for change thus leaving our people with only the armed struggle as the sole and legitimate means to attain its liberation...

The FDR proposed peace talks along the following lines:

1. The talks should be carried out between the delegates appointed by the FMLN/FDR and representatives of the junta of El Salvador.

2. They should be carried out in the presence of other governments that, as witnesses, will contribute to the solution of the conflict.

3. The nature of the talks must be general and include the fundamental aspects of the conflict. They must be based on an agenda established by both parties.

4. The Salvadoran people should be informed of the entire process.

5. They should be initiated without pre-established conditions by either party.

Prior to this proposal for negotiations, we had witnessed the Mexican-French declaration. The foreign ministers of Mexico and France, Jorge Castaneda and Claude Cheysson, jointly proclaimed:

1. Recognition of the FMLN/FDR alliance as a "representative political force ready to assure the obligations and exercise the rights that derive from that representation.

2. The alliance may legitimately participate in the necessary "rapprochement and negotiations toward a political solution to the crisis."

3. That the international community should facilitate the coming together of representatives of the political forces in conflict.

And what was the response to the Mexican/French declaration? Even in the face of fierce pressure by the United States government to ignore or denounce the Mexican/French declaration, numerous governments, parliaments, and international organizations expressed their agreement, or refrained from criticism. For example, Equador indicated that it favored a political solution and received a delegation from the FDR/FMLN. President Belaunde Terry of Peru indicated that a negotiated solution was in order. Costa Rica expressed its respect for the Mexican/French declaration. Panama rejected the notion that the Mexican/French declaration was in any way interventionist and noted that the only clear and undeniable intervention was being perpetrated by those governments providing military supplies and advisors in a clear reference to the U.S. role in that country. The United Nations Human Rights Sub-Committee meeting in Geneva voted to congratulate the French and Mexican governments in their initiative to recognize the FDR/FMLN as a legitimate political force in El Salvador. The vote was twenty-two in favor and one against. In an unexpected development, the European Parliament approved the Mexican-French declaration with broad support from its Christian Democratic members. The Socialist International unanimously approved the declaration. Finally, the Inter-Parliamentary Union, an international organization with a membership representing the Parliaments of over one hundred nations, expressed overwhelming approval of the declaration.

Many of the governments which endorsed the Mexican/French initiative have since been replaced by more conservative, pro-U.S. parties. Under unremitting pressure from Washington, the French government backed away from further involvement in Central American diplomacy and from significant aid to the Nicaraguan government. More recently, the U.S. government was publicly supportive and privately perturbed by the talks between the Duarte government and the FMLN/FDR at La Palma. Duarte has not responded to further FMLN/FDR proposals for peace talks. The U.S. clearly believes that the Salvadoran military can win the war on the battlefield.

Obviously we can have international law and order. We can have peace if we listen to the nations of the world. It is obvious that the future of Central America should not be decided by an isolated and extremist administration like Reagan's. If we establish a new international economic order, we can have the magnificent potential for world government which the United Nations offers if we can agree on its jurisdiction.

Another Vietnam?

There are many parallels between the situation in Central America today and the Indochina War. First of all, the use of covert and overt U.S. military aid to a repressive and unpopular military dictatorship. In the case of Vietnam there was General Ngo Dihn Diem, and then in the case of El Salvador there was aid to General Humberto Romero. I remember Diem, because he lived with us at our Maryknoll seminary until his return to Indochina. But the analogy in comparing and contrasting his position as an ineffectual person with that of General Humberto Romero in El Salvador I think is acceptable, notwithstanding his devout Catholicism. Second, both regimes were overthrown—Diem was assassinated—and replaced by more brutal military dictatorships through CIA-led military coups with the intention of derailing mounting opposition to the tyrannical regimes. In Vietnam we could mark November 1, 1963 as the moment that occurred. In El Salvador, October 15, 1979.

Point three in this comparison is the creation of a broad, massive coalition to oppose the new military dictatorship. In Vietnam this occurred through the formation of the National Liberation Front and in El Salvador it occurred through the formation of the Democratic Revolutionary Front, which literally includes hundreds of organizations of Salvadoran people.

Point number four is an increase in U.S. economic aid and military hardware to the dictatorship and of U.S. military personnel to train government troops and to lead them in search-and-destroy missions in the countryside. This certainly occurred in Indochina and is currently taking place in El Salvador.

Point number five is White House denials that U.S. military people are involved in combat, whether by leading troops or flying helicopters and planes. Washington insists that U.S. military personnel are now only there for advisory and training purposes, despite eyewitness reports to the contrary. We began to get these reports in Vietnam by 1963; we began to get them in El Salvador in 1980. We must keep in mind that the State Department is not a credible source. In terms of the past thirty years in Latin America, it would not have been useful to believe any of the comments of the White House on major issues. The White House lied about its role in the overthrow of the Arbenz regime in Guatemala in 1954. It lied about its role in the Bay of Pigs invasion in Cuba in 1961. It lied about its role in the overthrow of Juan Bosch of the Dominican Republic in 1965. It lied about its role in the overthrow of President Goulart in Brazil in 1962. It lied about its role in the overthrow of Chilean President Salvador Allende in 1973. This is all a matter of record. Clearly, we do not have a credible source in the U.S. Government—whether White House, State

Department, Pentagon, or CIA. Given such a record of deceit, better to assume a government statement is a lie and investigate it than to assume it must be truth and broadcast it.

The sixth point of comparison would be identification of the clergy with the popular movement, opposition to the government, and brutal repression against the Church in both countries. We saw this in the case of both Buddhists and Catholics in Indochina. In El Salvador such repression has been principally aimed against Catholics, because the vast majority of the people are Catholics. Progressive priests have been killed, the archbishop has been killed, sisters have been killed, all of this with tax money from people of the United States. We have another analogy with Vietnam: implementation of a U.S. conceived "land to the tiller" program under the guidance of Professor Roy Prosterman, both in El Salvador and in Vietnam, as a conduit for massive counterinsurgency and repression in the countryside. In Vietnam the death squad program was called "Operation Phoenix," and was one of the most bloodthirsty programs in that entire bloodthirsty war. The Salvadoran land reform is being sold as the most effective land reform program in the history of Latin America. It is not. It is a total fraud and a total failure. In fact, successful humane land reform in Central America wins not applause but intervention from U.S. policy-makers, as in our intervention to overthrow Arbenz in Guatemala years ago.

Point number seven is the determination of the people in both countries to carry on their struggle for national liberation for an indefinite time. The Vietnamese were prepared to fight for the rest of their lives, and their children would have fought for the rest of *their* lives. The situation is the same in Central America. The position of the people of El Salvador is irreversible; they have no intention of going back to slavery, under which they have lived for all of these decades. The legacy of U.S. control in El Salvador has been a legacy of malnutrition and illiteracy, and a total lack of social betterment. They will fight to end that condition.

The eighth point is the increasing regionalization of the conflict and the danger of an international conflagration. We know that this included South Vietnam, Laos, Cambodia, North Vietnam, and of course, the United States in the case of the Indochina War. As we look at Central America it certainly includes El Salvador, Guatemala, Honduras, Nicaragua, and of course, the United States. It is unfortunate that at this time Honduras is being used as a staging area for U.S. troops. Honduras has a common border with Guatemala, a common border with El Salvador, and a common border with Nicaragua.

The ninth point is opposition to U.S. intervention in Vietnam and in El Salvador by our strategic allies, which were or are under social democratic governments, such as France, Denmark, Norway, Sweden, Germany, Mexico, and others.

The tenth point in our comparison is internal opposition to United States intervention in El Salvador and Vietnam by different sectors of the American society—progressive, labor and university groups, Black and Latino populations—and a resistance to the draft in the United States.

For point eleven in this comparison, we see multinational economic interests in the resources of both regions, primarily oil and oil refining industries, shipping routes, and of course, cheap labor.

The final point is that of massive, direct U.S. military intervention in Vietnam in 1965, which leads us to ask the question: "Is this what we will see in Nicaragua and El Salvador in the 1980s?"

There is evident preoccupation in the military command about Latino members of the armed services serving in El Salvador, and about Black members serving in Africa. It is obvious that the military is conducting a great drive to find white bodies for cannon fodder. I noticed this very clearly on a 1985 visit to a local high school. I realized that before I had finished answering the first question, the vice principal was attempting to intervene to stop my explanation of the reality of El Salvador because she was afraid the five young men sitting in the back of the room, who had just joined the Marines, might understand the truth of the situation and not want to go. When she saw I was not about to yield the floor, she became very upset and went to call the principal of the high school. The principal began interrogating me and was literally twisting my arm, worrying perhaps that the high school would not be able to deliver. He ended up calling the security guard who escorted me off the campus.

I realized that this is a life and death fight. Young men sitting in those same high school seats went off to die in Indochina without knowing what they were fighting for, or who they were fighting and today men are signing up in the same fashion. I must admit I was quite angry, because I realized I really was fighting for the lives of those young men who were being kept in darkness. We will have to confront this reality in our public and private high schools. We do not want our youth going off to die out of malice or stupidity.

—7—
Conclusion

An unbroken thread extends from the sixties to the present. It goes from Central America to the U.S. around the rest of the world and back again to Central America. It is weaving a tapestry.

It would be extreme to say the Guatemalans were right in accusing us of plotting a revolution. In truth, however, we were not the strategists, we did not give orders. But yes, we were part of a current of thought and action. Such praxis is not limited to any one institution. It is not Vatican thought. It is not U.S. thought. It is the evolution of human thought. We were simply part of a mutation in theological orientation. It is not theory, it is theology in the doing.

Previously, it was considered important to define membership, to define creed, to think of religion as a scientific formula which could be memorized and recited. But liberation theology defines members by their conduct, as Jesus did. Liberation theology defines creed with scriptural universality and expansive acceptance. Those who have faith work to do the will of God on earth.

What is the value of discussing the virginity or lack of virginity of Mary? Shall we use our measured hours arguing about the divinity of Jesus? Shall we exhaust ourselves defining the Trinity? Of course not. We are called to renew the face of the earth. There is no place for the current governments of El Salvador, Guatemala, Honduras, or the United States in such a renewal.

Ask yourself, if Jesus were sitting in front of you, would you really want to discuss the virginity of his mother? Is that the issue? Would you not rather talk to him about making peace on earth? Why not talk to him about the future of Central America?

Guerrillas of peace are a vast army of people working for peace and justice. Some of them are members of churches. Some call themselves atheists. But all are humanists. They have developed a creed which does not have to be memorized. They know it! And they know each other.

109

Instinctively they work together in a process of observing, judging and acting. A new local entity is formed if nothing yet exists to do the job. By working and thinking (praying) together they network with other groups, seek consensus on issues, and express themselves through media. The goal is to restructure polities on every level: local, national, and international. The goal is to renew the face of the earth.

Guerrillas of peace have uncovered the reality of the common good. They have broken with the politics of the past, which is the art of how the few govern the many. No more governance by advertising. And no more fundamentalists. What is a fundamentalist? A fundamentalist is someone who is in love with the past and who is unfaithful to the past. The only way to be faithful to the past is not to repeat the mistakes of the past. Fidelity to the past is demonstrated by thoughtful change, change which breaks with past inhumanities. But fundamentalists of any sect will go on stoning adultresses, cutting off hands, practicing capital punishment, punishing the poor, and knowing that "they have the truth." They are self-condemned and they can be dangerous.

Hoping to avoid fundamentalist rhetoric, I suggest that guerrillas of peace can agree on the following: Oppression must be identified as the greatest evil. In a liberated society, health care is a right unrelated to a money economy. In an outdated, oppressive society, health care is bound to money. In a liberated society, education is a right unrelated to the money economy. Outdated, oppressive societies reserve education, especially so-called higher education, to the monied class.

The common good demands a minimum guaranteed income. Depending on the value of the dollar we might say $10,000 per year would be an acceptable minimum income. The common good also demands a ceiling on income, for example $150,000 per year. This does not kill incentive to work. Greatest achievements have been made by people with fixed incomes such as people on university salaries who do research and win Nobel prizes. Valid incentive comes from the achievement itself, excellence, legitimate income, and honors gained. How many mediocre physicians practicing one-minute medicine are now receiving salaries over $250,000 per year. If the incentive is simply to make money, we can be sure the performance will be the worst.

A new privileged class must be recognized. Human society can be gauged by the health, happiness, and comfort of this new privileged class. The class includes children, the aged, the sick, the mentally ill, refugees, and the homeless.

We do not accept the military model. There is no blind obedience. Leadership is won by being an example: "Let he or she who is great among you be as the servant of all."(Mark 10; 43) Individual or collective leadership must be in communion with the people and just a few steps ahead of them.

The nation state as the terminus of sovereignty is as outdated as the city states of old. International Law and Order is required. Had the decisions of the U.N. been given full jurisdiction there might have been no Indochina War. There would be no intervention in Central America. There would be no nuclear war. The U.N. design for a New International Economic Order is entirely logical. Am I speaking of World Federalism? Yes.

Guerrillas of peace are those who are willing to dedicate their lives, their fortunes, and their sacred honor to bringing about these changes. What are the instruments, the tools to be used by guerrillas of peace? First and foremost is education—political education. Political education includes an understanding of the oligarchy which runs the United States. The Metropolitan 400 made their undeserved wealth by making arms for the Civil War. The New Rich made their undeserved wealth from World Wars I and II. And now, with the permanent war economy of the United States, every available parasite is in the arms business. If "business is business," there is nothing but the arms business. If values are considered, it is the worst business.

Certainly the most desirable instrument of change is electoral politics. It is clean, easy, and occasionally fair. Unfortunately, electoral politics is currently giving us the best government that money can buy. Money must be removed from the electoral process. Candidates who qualify by collecting a given number of signatures should be given an equal amount of TV or radio time and equal access to the public. Quality would improve.

Unfortunately, most of the needed changes are not winnable at the ballot box under the current system. Much of the change must come about through mass mobilization and organization. This is expensive politics. It takes time and risk. Strikes and boycotts are useful tools. Demonstrations are of value if conducted with sound discipline and a clear distinction between those who intend to engage in civil disobedience and those who want to participate in the legal activities. The Pledge of Resistance Campaign to mobilize U.S. citizens to oppose U.S. intervention in Nicaragua and Central America generally is a powerful combination of legal protest and non-violent civil disobedience.

All forms of media are part of the battle. If the pen is mightier than the sword then the media is mightier than the sword. Use it. There is a battle for curriculum in public schools. That curriculum has been almost totally sterilized. In the U.S., the first thirteen years of schooling will include no study of socialism. Such study is even rare on our university campuses. Constructive change cannot take place if socialism is ignored. It takes more than rock concerts to eliminate world misery.

We will know we are getting somewhere when teachers and doctors have a similar modest income. We will know we are getting somewhere when lawyers and social workers have a similar modest income. Further gauges of success will be: low-cost housing, functional mass transit, extensive international student exchange, and U.N.-supervised disarmament.

Religious, political, and ethnic tags are almost valueless at this point in history. There are marxist murderers and there are Catholic murderers. One's background is of interest culturally. But polities of the future will not be built on such labels. "By their fruits you shall know them."

Guerrillas of peace are not neutral. There is no biblical neutrality. There is no neutrality in the face of injustice. We intend always to choose the side of justice and to systematize love. We will do so from within our respective cultures. We have no intention of promoting syncretism. Humanity is the measure.

How quickly people will accept the values of humanity over the mythological nonsense of advertising. Let the polity ask, "All those in favor of smog, please raise your hands?" How quickly we will understand that living in filthy air is not a price we have to pay for "development." This is not the price we have to pay for "jobs." On the contrary, the smog is nothing but a monument to the greed of the few. In the current system, to damage one persons lungs is a felony. To damage the lungs of ten million people living in a megalopolis is no crime at all. Personalistic morality is not the key to peace on earth.

There are many occupational hazards for aspiring guerrillas of peace. We have the luxury to seek new instruments of change so we will not have to use the traditional instruments of change. We are *not* the non-violent holy ones in the midst of the violent savages of Asia, Africa, and Latin America. A hazard of churchpeople is the presumption that somehow they are more moral than the Guatemalan rebels. They are not. They simply have not had the same pressures of the Guatemalan rebels.

It is hypocritical to condemn hostage-taking in Lebanon, while we pay taxes so all of Nicaragua can be taken hostage, or so that indiscriminate bombing can be conducted in El Salvador. We paid taxes and observed the battleship New Jersey shelling Shiite Villages in Lebanon (to the tune of the Star Spangled Banner). And we still wonder what they are angry about? Moral perfectionism is a hazard for people of religious background. Some will fall by the wayside saying, "I am waiting for the perfect program." They will never do anything.

People of strong political background must watch out for the hazard of dogmatic purity. Curious groups of U.S. socialists have been seen traveling around Nicaragua attempting to define whether this is or is not socialism. What a waste of time! Authentic revolutionaries are not dogmatists. They are people in process and they are reading the gauges of socialism in terms of social achievements.

Perhaps the most important quality of a guerrilla of peace is reverence. Reverence for the atheist who will not say the name of the Lord for fear of taking that name in vain. Reverence enough not to be telling people what God will or won't do. Reverence to believe in Providence. Look at the sand and look at the stars. Look at the atoms and look at the galaxies. Each worthy ripple has eternal value. The struggle itself is the school. It makes no difference who sees it. The struggle is more important than our life. It is far deeper than any one organization. It is a matter of renewing the earth and having the faith to know that whatever we do is eternal. Living fully in the present is to understand the eternal now.

Certainly there will be restrictions. The conflict between justice and liberty will continue. I would opt for no freedom for children to go hungry; no freedom for the mentally ill to live out of garbage cans; no freedom to oppress women and men in prostitution; no freedom to be illiterate; no freedom to die of polio, malaria an other curable diseases; no freedom to be without income; and little sympathy for those who in their misguided notion of liberty would continue to support the freedom of misery.

Guerrillas of peace are not individualist. They find themselves through interaction with their brothers and sisters. Organization begins locally and extends through networking—religious and secular organizations working together; literally thousands of local organizations are so much in sync that they see each other as branch offices; so much in consensus that we share the feelings of the peasant on the Island of Solentiname on the Lake of Nicaragua: "We all come to the same conclusions and we have not even met each other." How similar to, "And each heard in his or her own tongue."

The Peace March for Human Rights, Self-Determination and Solidarity in Central America provides an excellent example of international networking and action. Initiated in Norway, Peace March steering committees have been organized in the United States, El Salvador, Nicaragua, Costa Rica, Canada, Sweden, Denmark, Finland, and Great Britain. The Peace March—scheduled for December 10, 1985 through January 20, 1986—will travel through Panama, Costa Rica, Nicaragua, Honduras, El Salvador, Guatemala, and Mexico. People will be able to join the March for all or part of the journey, or participate in support events in their home communities. Two key objectives of the Peace March are to establish permanent cooperation among the participants in Central America and around the world, and to support the Contadora peace proposals.

Jesus was not a sectarian. Sectarianism annoyed him. He wanted all to be as one. Let the spirituality of this movement become clear. The first step in spirituality is to accept one human family, one race, the human race. As this familial view of society becomes clear, we can begin to say, "Abba...Father," or "Mother," if you wish.

From the first step proceeds the second concept. "Might makes Right" (imperialism) is not compatible with authentic spirituality. We cannot serve two masters. We must not have strange gods. We must not make an idol out of the nation.

The third level of spirituality includes an active solidarity with our brothers and sisters everywhere. The millions of hungry children in New York City are my children. And so are the ones in Ethiopia. What I would do for my own children, I must do for them. And I can only do it through intensive commitment and organization.

Living in misery is an evil. Attaining frugality, on the other hand, is a desirable achievement. By frugality I mean that condition where people have a sufficiency of goods and services, a sufficiency of study, culture, formal education, and leisure. Bringing the Third World and the poor of the U.S. to the level of frugality would be an achievement indeed.

Many references to "the poor" lack specificity. We must not glorify the condition falsely. Some of the poor have no concept of their own class and would easily be unfaithful to their class. Some poor people will accept a role as Death Squad members. I am sure it is possible for a religious person to live "with the poor" for her or his entire life and only confirm the continuation of poverty. Living with the poor, as Mother Theresa does, does not imply political change. It may only lead to more Mother Theresas and more poverty. "The poor you always have with you" was not a mandate. It was an observation of Jesus about the reality of his time.

Now that we have opened a vast market with China, it is a little difficult to identify "International Communism" as the devil. Thus, a new devil has been created. It is called "International Terrorism." "International Terrorism" has even less reality than "International Communism."

Agencies of government, like commercials, generally speak with absolute contempt for the listener. The explanation of "International Terrorism" goes something like this: "There is a man. And this man's name is Carlos. He lives in South America. Carlos is the father of International Terrorism. He has been seen in Europe and the United States. Anyone with information about the whereabouts of Carlos, please call your local FBI." Infantilism is a requirement for listening to government propaganda.

There are homicidal maniacs, of course. And every precaution is necessary to avoid innocent victims. But many "terrorist" acts must be seen as acts of war, and we have to be ready to compare what the terrorists have done with what our government has done. Did we avoid civilian casualties when we A-bombed Hiroshima? Or Nagasaki? Either we should include such acts in the conception of "International Terrorism," or we should drop the scheme.

Much of what I have learned has come from experiences (Guatemala), from the Savior (El Salvador), and from that victory won with humanity and reverence (Nicaragua). I am always moved by the absence of bitterness in the authentic revolutionary. How calmly they explain to U.S. audiences that their harbors have been mined, their citizens raped and murdered, and their revolution maligned by lies, lies, and more lies of U.S. origin. There is a clear distinction between a revolutionary and a bitter person. Spiteful, vindictive, mean-spirited people are everywhere. They are not revolutionaries. The anger must not be personal. Anger, like the solution, must be systemic.

We must try not to get in the way of our message. How futile is the legitimate cry of Black people if their anger is directed at the white race. How dull the legitimate message of feminists if their anger is directed at men in the abstract. How weak the cry for socialism if it becomes a personal attack on people who work hard, support their families, yet who have only lived with capitalism. I know I have failed many times in communication because my anger has been misinterpreted as personal. I am trying to learn. Hundreds of thousands of U.S. visitors have been been to Cuba and Nicaragua. They are met with respect and affection. "Imperialismo Yanqui" is a reference to U.S. foreign policy, not to the people of the United States. I wish U.S. citizens also knew that. I can still hear Paul Goodman saying, "Anger is healthy, but spite is sick." Are we angry? Yes.

We are at war with the military budget. We are at war with nerve gas. We are at war with MX missiles. We are at war with binary shells. We are at war with nuclear submarines. We are at war with the U.S. occupation of Europe, Asia, Africa, and Latin America. We are at war with nuclear war. We are at war with illiteracy. We are at war with the draft in any nation not under physical attack. We are at war with capital punishment and 16th-century-style prisons. We are at war with torture. We are at war with intervention. We are at war with war. We do not defend or wish to repeat the history of the Soviet Union. We wish to acknowledge its achievements and question its errors. Repeating the past is not our objective. Creating the future is our objective.

We can choose the way of mythology (lies) or the way of truth. Mythology leads to Reaganism, where truth is whatever one says it is, whatever works to one's personal advantage or profit. Much of world culture has been based upon this type of truth, so evident in the barbarism of history.

Guerrillas of peace share in the heritage of the U.S. revolution of 1776. We do not represent the founders by waving flags and burping out "Nuke Em!" at any pretended foe. The arms race is a con game designed to put U.S. tax money into the pockets of irresponsible and incompetent parasites who have drained this country dry. The arms

race is not for defense, it is not for freedom, it is not for democracy. It is
for profit. We started the arms race at Hiroshima. We must stop it.

Guerrillas of peace are intelligent patriots. We want Old Glory
and we want it to wave with all the flags of the United Nations. We are
guerrillas of peace because we are in love with children and all people,
we are in love with peace, we are in love with justice, we are in love
with creating a political system based on love and respect, we are in
love with play and celebration.

The model for this great new world is simplicity, a dialogical
family, women and men creating and caring. A society good for children will be good for everyone. Revolución, si. Revolution, yes. Hasta la
victoria siempre! Forever forward until victory!

FOOTNOTES

Introduction

1. Blase Bonpane, "The Church in the Central American Revolution," *Thought*, Vol. 59, No. 233, June 1984, Fordham University Quarterly, pp. 183-194.
2. Walter LaFeber, *Inevitable Revolutions* (New York, W. W. Norton and Company, 1983) pp. 170-71.
3. Jonathan Kwnitny, *Endless Enemies* (New York, Congdon & Weed, Inc. 1984) p. 275.
4. T. D. Allman, *Unmanifest Destiny* (New York, The Dial Press, 1984) pp. 1-18.
5. Pope John XXIII, *Mater et Magistra and Pacem in Terris* (Washington, D.C.: National Catholic Welfare Conference, 1961.)
6. Manuel Aguirre and Jesus Rodriguez, *Cursillos de Capacitación Social* (Panama: Centro de Capacitación Social, 1965.)
7. Thomas and Marjorie Melville, *Guatemala, The Politics of Land Ownership* (New York: The Free Press, 1971).
8. Augusto C. Sandino, *Pensamientos* (Managua: Comite Democratico Nueva Nicaragua, 1979), p. 14.
9. *Centro de Capacitación Social*, Archivos, (Guatemala, 1966.)
10. Ibid.
11. Ibid.
12. Ibid.
13. Blase A. Bonpane, "A Priest on Guatemala," *The Washington Post*, February 4, 1968.
14. Herbert Aptheker, *The Urgency of Marxist-Christian Dialogue* (New York: Harper and Row, 1970), pp. 2-8.
15. Susanne Jonas and David Tobias, *Guatemala* (New York: North American Congress On Latin America, 1974).
16. See note 6.
17. Letter of Ernesto Cardenal, December 1968.
18. Hugo Assman, *Habla Fidel Castro Sobre Los Cristianos Revolucionarios* (Montevideo: Tierra Neuva, 1972), p. 40.
19. *Latin America Press*, Lima, Peru, September 13, 1979.
20. Carlos, A Nicaraguan campesino.
21. Blase Bonpane, "A letter to Pope John Paul II," *Los Angeles Weekly*, March 24, 1983.
22. Assman, *Habla Fidel Castro* p. 7.
23. Archbishop Oscar Arnulfo Romero, Cathedral of San Salvador, July 29, 1979.
24. Pope John Paul II, *Evangelii Nuntiandi*.

Chapter One

1. Blase Bonpane reviews *Churches and Politics in Latin America, Journal of Church and State*, Volume 23, Number 1, Winter 1981, pp. 131-32.
2. Blase Bonpane, "The Church and Revolutionary Struggles in Central America," *Latin America Perspectives*, Volume VII, Numbers 2 and 3, Spring and Summer of 1980, pp. 178-189.
3. Manuel Aguirre and Jesus Rodrigues Jalon, Cursillos de Capacitación Social (Panama: Centro de Capacitatión Social).
4. Centro de Capacitation Social, Archives, Guatemala, 1966.
5. Pablo Richard, ed., Historia de la Teologia en America Latina, Departmento Ecumenico de Investigaciones, San Jose, Costa Rica.
6. J. Andrew Kirk, *Liberation Theology* (Atlanta: John Knox Press, 1979) p. 29, ff.
7. Ibid. p. 160.
8. Carolyn Cook Dipboye, "The Roman Catholic Church and the Political Struggle for Human Rights in Latin America. 1969-1980," pp. 497-524.
9. Blase Bonpane, "A Priest on Guatemala," *Washington Post*, Feb. 4, 1968.
10. Centro de Capacitación Social, Archives, Guatèmala, 1966.
11. Blase Bonpane, "Our Latin Vietnam," *Los Angeles Times*, February 11, 1968.
12. *Centroamerica: Cristianismo y Revolucion*, Cuadernos number 4, Departmento Ecumenico de Investigaciones, San Jose, Costa Rica, 1980.
13. Jorge V. Pixley, "Lecturas Biblicas Latinamericanas," *Taller de Teologia*, Numero 8, 1981, Editorial Gubani, Mexico, D.F. pp. 5-15.
14. Paulo Freire, *Pedogogy of the Oppressed* (New York: Herder and Herder, 1968).
15. Blase Bonpane, "A Priest and the Student Guerrillas," *Look*, April 29, 1969.
16. Blase Bonpane, "Guerrillas of Peace," *Boston Sunday Globe*, September 22, 1968.
17. Thomas and Margie Melville, *Guatemala: The Politics of Land Ownership* (New York, The Free Press, 1971).
18. Centro de Capacitación Social, Archives, Guatemala, 1967.
19. Eduardo Galeano, *Guatemala: Pais Ocupado* (Editorial Nuestro Tiempo, 1967).
20. Centro de Capacitación Social, Archives, Guatemala, 1967.

Chapter Two

1. Blase Bonpane, "In Beleaguered Guatemala, Long Suffering Indians Join the Opposition," March 23, 1980.
2. Uriel Molina, *Las Iglesias en la Practica de la Justicia*, Departmento Ecumenico de Invesitigaciones, San Jose, Costa Rica, 1981, p 49 ff

3. *The Jerusalem Bible* (New York, Doubleday, 1966) p. 56-7.
4. Ibid. p. 669.
5. Matthew 10, 16.
6. Pablo Richard, "Identidad eclesial en la practica politica, organia y teorica del movimiento popular," *Cristianismo y Sociedad*, Numero 67, 1981, Editorial Tierra Nueva, Republica Dominicana, p. 15 ff.
7. R. Egenter, *Ueber die Bedeutung der Epikie Imsittlichen Liben*, in Phil. Jahrb, 1940, pp. 115-127. Bernard Haring, *Tugend der Epikie*, in die Gegenwartige Heilsstunde, pp. 210-218.
8. Hugo Assman, "La fe de los pobres en lucha contra los idolos," *La Lucha de Los Dioses*, Centro Antonio Valdvieso, Managua, Nicaragua, 1980.
9. Mathew 5, 39.

Chapter Three

1. Hugo Zorrilla, *La Fiesta de Liberacion de los Oprimidos* (San Jose, Costa Rica Ediciones Sebila) pp 247 ff.
2. St. Thomas Aquinas, *Summa Theologica*, Volume II, p. 1994, New York, Benziger Brothers, 1947.
3. Leslie Dewart, *Christianity and Revolution* (New York, Herder and Herder, 1963), pp. 103-115.
4. *The Jerusalem Bible*, New York, Doubleday, 1966, p. 31.
5. Ibid., p. 27.
6. Ibid., p. 181.
7. *Carta Enciclica de su Santidad el Papa Pablo VI Sobre El Desarrollo de los Pueblos*, Sec. 31, Emiliani, San Salvador, 1967.
8. Luke 16, 21.
9. Penny Lernoux, *Cry of the People* (New York, Doubleday, 1980) p. 56 ff.
10. Ibid. p. 117 ff.
11. *Camilo Torres: Biografia-Plataforma-Mansajes* (edellin, Columbia, Ediciones Carpel-Antorcha, M, 1966).
12. Roberto Oliveros, *Liberacion y Teologia* (Lima, Peru, Centro de Estudios y Publicaciones, 1980) pp. 121-25.
13. *The Jerusalem Bible* (New York, Doubleday, 1966) p. 118.
14. Ibid. p. 306.
15. Ibid. pp. 384-85.
16. Ibid. p. 54.
17. Blase Bonpane, *Los Angeles Times*, "In Beleaguered Guatemala, Long-Suffering Indians Join the Opposition," March 23, 1980.
18. Hugo Assman, *Habla Fidel Castro Sobre los Cristianos Revolucionaries* (Montevideo, Tierra Nueva, 1972).
19. *The Jerusalem Bible* (New York, Doubleday, 1966) p. 1514.
20. Ibid. p. 53.

Afterword

The rich and the powerful are wrong about 90 percent of the time. They are morally wrong because their lives are focused on protecting their power and money. Lies and violence are their methodology. But certainly they can become traitors to their class and as such we welcome them.

War is the conventional tool of the rich and powerful. Centuries of skill have taught them how to enlist the young and the poor to fight their patriotic battles.

Neither the United States nor the rest of the world should continue to exist with the current maldistribution of wealth. Fifteen years ago the top 1 percent of the families of the United States held 27 percent of the wealth. Today they hold 36 percent of the nation's wealth. Greed is simply not an acceptable motor for a just economy. The Reagan administration has demonstrated this reality with great clarity.

If we look at the lowest 20 percent of U.S. families, they are now earning one-third less than they were fifteen years ago. This means that one out of five children in the United States is hungry. This means that two out of every five Hispanic and three out of every five black children are hungry. Jobs available during the Reagan administration are an invitation to perpetual poverty. Most of these jobs are below the poverty level of $180 per week. Hence a fulltime worker might earn enough to pay his or her landlord and have nothing left to purchase food.

But the unity of the human race is beginning to assert itself. Guerrillas of peace are an irreversible reality. I am personally grateful for having experienced the power of such democratic currents:

in the organization of base communities in Central America,
in the Peace Movement of the Indochina War,
in the organizing of the United Farm Workers' movement in
    the United States
in the movement against nuclear weapons and power,
in the international efforts to stop the U.S. war in Central
    America.

121

Regarding this latter issue, it is necessary to mention the International March for Peace in Central America. Three hundred people from thirty countries marched from Panama to Mexico in support of the Contadora Peace Process and self-determination for Central America. In the wake of this march, many participants remained to serve as internationalists in Nicaragua, El Salvador, Honduras, and Guatemala. U.S. press censorship was clearly identified as journalists marched with us, filed their stories only to see almost every report "killed" by editors at the home base. We were able to see the impact of billions of dollars spent to control Central America by sheer terror and brutality. We were able to understand the relationship between this waste and the dismal domestic conditions in the United States. We were physically attacked by pro-contra fascists called Costa Rica Libre. Indeed the revulsion of Costa Rican citizens at the violence of this group was so great that the scales were tipped away from the popular pro-contra candidate and the more progressive Oscar Arias was elected. After demonstrating at Fort Howard in Panama, witnessing the devastation of the contra-mercenary-terrorists in Nicaragua and conducting missions of accompaniment in El Salvador and Guatemala, we arrived in Mexico City and were joined by the largest outpouring of Mexican citizens seen in a decade. Finally marchers formed the International Network for Peace in Central America to maintain active communications between all of the Central American countries and the United States.

Another memorable example was the Search for Peace Conference in El Salvador. One hundred and seventy-five of us arrived in that tortured country to engage in peace talks in spite of the wishes of the Salvadoran government and the U.S. Embassy (the current capital of El Salvador). Hundreds of Salvadorans met us at the Catholic University to express their plans for peace. Church, union, peasant, student, professional and political leaders welcomed the initiative. We branched out through the countryside speaking to rebels and members of the military.

The need for ongoing resistance has become obvious. It is not enough to be "in session" only on special days. No group has given a better example on this matter than the great Vietnam veterans who began the Veterans Fast for Life. Their initial forty-seven day fast led directly to the formation of the Veterans Peace Action Teams and marches through the ugliest contra war zones of Nicaragua. Other teams have followed to rebuild what our tax money has destroyed.

As veterans open their projects to all people of good will yet another dimension is in development, the World Peace Force. This concept was born on the railroad tracks in front of the Naval Weapons Station at Port Chicago, California. Some 2,000 of us blockaded the entrance of this nefarious base from which the material of death finds its way to El Salvador, Honduras and the contras. While barricades were built on the tracks, while veterans spoke of peace and Marine

Guards listened, while over two hundred were arrested, while Alice Walker spoke, the Veterans Peace Action Team remained at the tracks to recruit an ongoing presence. Weeks later, the veterans are still at the tracks each day. I believe this new presence will become the World Peace Force and that it will operate in the United States, Central America or anywhere else on earth where it might be needed.

> If liberty and democracy are to be truly saved, they will only be by non-violent resistance no less brave, no less glorious than violent resistance. And it will be infinitely braver and more glorious because it will give life without taking any.
> —Mahatma Ghandi

These peace making ventures must be the mark of the end of this century of war. Those who continue to identify and use these new instruments of change are worthy of the title, Guerrillas of Peace.

It is not necessarily the most dangerous projects that are the most effective. It is not necessarily those who are arrested most often or those who fast unto death. "I don't want to be a Peace Rambo," said one of the most dedicated members of the Veterans Peace Action Team.

It is the most meaningful projects that will be most effective. This includes careful thought, planning, discernment and finally action, such as exemplified by the recent Office of the Americas Teen Delegation to Nicaragua led by Theresa and Colleen Bonpane. Here was a chemistry between people that other efforts had not generated. Commercial media responded. U.S. teens built a bond with Nicaraguan teens. The U.S. teens will never look upon Nicaragua as "the enemy."

If there are any heroes in this work let them be identified as that army of self-effacing volunteers who do the menial tasks of addressing and stamping envelopes. Any organized effort would be impossible without them.

Once base communities form, there is an electricity of communication on matters pertaining to practice. There is a collective genius. (For an example of base communities in the United States, see Directory of Central America Organizations, 1987, Central America Resource Center, P.O. Box 2327, Austin, Texas 78768.) It was thrilling to hear a stodgy member of Congress list prominent U.S. solidarity organizations during the Contragate hearings. Apparently some members of the legislative branch are beginning to understand that we do not consider ourselves to be petitioners of government. On the contrary, we are expressing direction and leadership. Servants in office must respond.

Electoral politics are not to be ignored. I have as much respect for people who try to run an effective campaign oriented toward the liberation of the poor as I do for marchers who are faced off against the Honduran Cobras (elite forces). Dogmatists often make the mistake of trying to identify the one way of political action. There is not one way; there are many ways.

Simultaneous with working to restructure the entire body politic we must not lose interest in the best legislation and the best candidates. And political sins must be punished. For example, any person in elective or appointive office who has supported the contra-mercenary-terrorists against the people of Nicaragua should be targeted for defeat. He or she is not fit to serve.

But much of our work will only be accomplished through mass mobilization. We can continue to learn from the poor of the earth. Unbelievable examples of courage have come to us from the Koreans, the Filipinos, the South Africans, the Salvadorans, the Guatemalans, the Hondurans. All of these great mobilizers have proven to us the need for weeks, months and years of street action.

Such political consciousness will lead to the formation of a political party of the majority in the United States. Currently we have what can be described as a one-party system of corporate capital which has two facets: the Republicans and the Democrats. We deserve something better. Once our national ideology of anti-communism is destroyed we will be able to destroy the dope trade and organized crime. We will also be able to take pride in some of our representatives.

We can deal with the demands of distributive justice and disallow the 1 percent their policy-making power and their organized theft. We might call it the Majority Party. Once politically conscious, the majority of U.S. citizens will welcome such a solution.

In the meantime, we desperately need Nicaragua. Note the wisdom of the eminient Professor Donald Bray as recorded in the *Los Angeles Times* (6/22/87):

> Congress should evaluate the Sandinista revolution in Nicaragua in its world context. It is part of an historical process advanced in 1968 when Czech leader Alexander Dubcek attempted to implement "socialism with a human face."
>
> Dubcek's and three other similar experiments have been ended with help from the superpowers: Poland's Solidarity, Grenada's New Jewel Movement, and Salvador Allende's Chile.
>
> "Human face" socialism seems to make superpowers nervous. (Though it may be too early to judge the post-Mikhail Gorbachev U.S.S.R. on this issue.) All the world has left of this kind of polity is Nicaragua. Nicaragua's new constitution combines the political guarantees of the West with the social and economic rights of the East, making the country an important bridge between the two systems.
>
> Instead of trying to destroy it, we should declare the Nicaraguan government an endangered political species and take measures to preserve it.

Postscript to the Second Edition by Father Ernesto Cardenal Minister of Culture of Nicaragua

Jesus is still being persecuted by the pharisees and sadducees. They cannot keep him quiet so they try to make people believe that he said the opposite of what he really said.

When he said, "How happy are the poor in spirit," (Matthew 5, 3) they said he referred to the ones who were not materially poor, only spiritually poor meaning the good rich. It is as if Jesus had said, "Happy are the rich." But we know that Jesus used the Hebrew word *anawim* (the poor of Yahweh) which does not have a translation in Greek. He was referring to the poor of Israel who were waiting for their liberation. It would be the same if he had said, "Happy are the people of the Third World." Matthew could not translate this into Greek so he used "poor in spirit." Jesus was talking about the poor, the really poor. This is clear when Luke says in his passage on the beatitudes, "How happy are you who are poor," (Luke 6, 20). What is more, after the beatitudes he adds curses for the rich. The rich are not condemned because they are bad rich, but because they are rich.

In Hebrew literature parallelism is often used. They say the same thing twice with some variation of words. Here in the beatitudes Jesus uses multiple parallelism. All the happy ones are the same people with different names. And all the rewards are the same with different names.

The happy ones are:

The poor, the gentle, those who mourn, those who hunger and thirst for what is right, the merciful, those who are pure in heart, the peacemakers, those who are persecuted for the cause of right.

And they are happy because:

Theirs is the kingdom of heaven; they shall have the earth for their heritage; they shall be comforted; they shall be satisfied; they shall have mercy shown them; they shall see God; they shall be called sons of God; theirs is the kingdom of heaven.

Here we can see that the ones mentioned at the end, the persecuted, have the same reward as the ones mentioned first, the poor; the kingdom of heaven belongs to them.

If the ones mentioned at the beginning, "the poor in spirit" were materially rich we would need an abundant imagination to think that these rich are also those who are gentle, those who mourn, those who hunger and thirst for what is right, the merciful, those who are pure in heart, the peacemakers, and those who are persecuted for the cause of right. All of this would be possible if they would no longer be rich.

There are also curses to the rich which Luke writes after the beatitudes. After he blesses the poor, Jesus adds these curses: "Woe to you rich..." (Luke 6, 24). The rich are cursed because they have had their happiness, because they are satisfied, because they laugh now, because everyone worldly speaks well of them. They are not condemned because they are bad rich but because they are rich.

This is similar to the parable of poor Lazarus (Luke 16, 19-31) and rich Dives. Lazarus is saved simply because he is poor while the other is rich. It does not say he was rewarded for any other virtue, not even for his patience. But the rich man, Dives, is condemned for being rich.

Therefore what is bad is that there are rich and poor. It is not bad that there are riches on earth for people to enjoy; these riches have been created by God or by people. What is bad is that some can enjoy them and some cannot. As Saint Paul said, "It is a matter of share and share alike. At present your plenty should supply their need and then at some future date their plenty may supply your need" (2 Corinthians 8, 14). The early christians lived this equality.

Frederick Engels wrote that the first Christian communities were the inspiration of modern revolutionary movements. Most social change comes from the Bible, the writings which Jesus said he did not come to destroy but to fulfill (Matthew 5, 17).

Some philosophers believe that social injustice is inevitable. Aristotle said that slavery was necessary. But the prophets of the bible announced a total change in society. And Christ brought good news to the poor: the announcement that the kingdom of God was beginning and that it was for them.

People from rich societies must show solidarity with poor societies even when they are geographically distant. (Many movements and organizations make this possible.) The above mentioned reference to Saint Paul is his plea for the affluent Greeks to help the poor of Jerusalem.

Following this example, there will not be rich and poor because all the riches of nature and of people will be shared by all. Then the scriptures will be fulfilled even to the Apocalypse. The Apocalypse is a frequently misused word. It does not mean the next (and last) world war—the explosion of all the megatons. It means the death of the beast, the fall of Babylon, the triumph of good over evil, the new society coming down from heaven, the day when every tear will be dry.

People have accused me of saying that heaven would be on earth and therefore I have denied the resurrection. Certainly I believe that heaven will be on earth. Saint Matthew, following the Jewish tradition, does not mention the name of God. What Matthew calls the kingdom of heaven, the other three evangelists call the kingdom of God. But this does not mean the kingdom of God will be up in the sky. The kingdom of God is a perfect and happy society that will be established on earth.

Christ came to announce the beginning of this kingdom, a kingdom that was beginning with him. And in the Lord's Prayer he taught us to ask that the kingdom come to us, not that we go to the kingdom. Jesus promises the kingdom of heaven to the poor but he promises that the gentle will have the earth for their heritage. Are the poor and the gentle going to have such different rewards? Do these words of Jesus not indicate that heaven and earth are the same?

The main message of Jesus, the good news, is the announcement of the kingdom. Christ also talked about resurrection. He related this resurrection, the victory over death, to the establishment of the kingdom on earth. Therefore I believe that the Christian must also believe in resurrection.

Christ said, "Unless a wheat grain falls on the ground and dies, it remains only a single grain; but if it dies, it yields a rich harvest" (John 12, 24). I often think about those grains of wheat in the tombs of the Pharaohs. Such grains have not died yet, but neither have they reproduced. Death and resurrection; this mystery was in the ancient religions. It was the main topic in the mysteries of Eleusis where it was explained to the beginners by showing them an ear of wheat. This is why Christ chose wheat for the mystery of the eucharist, the memorial of his death and resurrection.

In order to resurrect our life, life has to be given away not only individually but societally. As individuals, we have to let die the capitalism that is inside each of us, the selfishness. Sandino's flag was red and black. Sandino said that black meant death and red meant resurrection. Our people have known death and they have known much suffering and now they also know resurrection.

It has been said that what separates Christians from marxists is the belief that there is life after death. But marxists also believe that one who dies for the people lives on. A Nicaraguan bishop was amazed when I told him that atheist marxists also believe in the resurrection. they cannot explain clearly how the person lives on but we cannot explain the resurrection either.

We know, however, that we rise because Christ told Martha and she believed that we would rise on the last day but this did not console her. "I know that he [Lazarus] will rise again at the resurrection on the last day" (John 11, 25). Then Jesus explained that the resurrection is now.

We also know that we will not rise with the same body we now have. Christ affirmed this while speaking to the Sadducees stating that there will be no sex, that we will be "like angels" without organs or biological functions. When Christ came out of his tomb, he was different than before. Magdalene thought he was a gardener. And when he appeared to his disciples, they did not recognize him. He had to tell them who he was.

How does the resurrection take place? During the gospel commentaries with the peasants of Solentiname a young man, Donald, said, "I don't think we will rise in a material form. The things that will rise will be the conscience and the love the person had. This way we will not have the odd situation of skeletons walking around." We all roared with laughter. Donald was later assassinated by Somoza's National Guard. We have unearthed his bones and placed them under a monument. But now he is not only bones.

A young peasant named Elvis said on another occasion, "I think the risen are those who lived and died for the people like Camilio Torres and Che Guevara. They are alive; they are a living force for the people." Elvis was also assassinated. His bones are beside Donald's. But now he is not bones either. Another young man from Solentiname recently wrote a poem to Elvis saying that he is alive in the laughter of the children who run and sing, healthy in the meadows of our land.

In our times we cannot visualize resurrection like they did in the paintings of the middle ages: the bones being covered with flesh again. That is even more difficult for the ones who do not even have bones anymore. I imagine it in a different way. My explanation is more poetic than theological or scientific. We will rise in a material way but with another kind of material. We will be the conscience of the universe. And our body will be the whole universe. There will be only one body for all of us and only one conscience. This way we will be united to God who is in the whole universe, in space and if there is something beyond space, beyond the fourth dimension of space beyond time.

But first we must establish the kingdom, perfect justice on earth. An atheistic marxist from Spain said that he didn't understand why Christians do not believe that selfishness would ever disappear when they believe in something much more difficult such as the resurrection of the body. Actually, St. Paul said that the last enemy to be defeated will be death. Therefore selfishness will be defeated before death. Teilhard de Chardin said that we can never anticipate sufficiently the growing human unity.

I believe the prophecy of Isaiah 65, 21-24 will be fulfilled:

They will build houses and inhabit them,
plant vineyards and eat their fruit.
They will not build for others to live in,
or plant so that others can eat.
For my people shall live as long as trees,
and my chosen ones wear out what their hands

have made. They will not toil in vain or beget
children to their own ruin...

For us Christians our life has to continue beyond this planet. If it
didn't the revolution would end here. If it didn't the final victory would
be the victory of the status quo. As a Mexican theologian said, "The
final victory would be death. The final victory would be Reagan's."

We are heaven for any other planet where the inhabitants observe
us in the starry night. I believe in heaven. And I believe that heaven is
in this planet and everywhere. The kingdom of God will be established
here. We will rise in this kingdom.

Index

Hitler, Adolf, 89
Holy Orders, 17
Honduras, 91, 106, 109, 113
Honolulu, 64
Huehuetenango, 25-28, 39, 60, 66
Human Rights Commission of El
  Salvador, 97

Immerman, Richard, 27
imperialism, 15, 114, 115
Indochina, 106, 107
  war in, 19, 105, 111
Inter-Parliamentary Union, 104

Jefferson, Thomas, 98
Jesuits, 2
Jews, 86
John Paul II, Pope, 10, 13, 19, 91
John XXIII, Pope, 2
Johnson, Lyndon Baines, 73
Joyabaj, El Quiche, 43
Judeo-Christian values, 94
Juil, 43

Khomeini, Ayatollah, 86
Kinzer, Stephen, 27
Korea, 103
Kurds, 86

La Libertad, 26
La Mano Blanco, 28-30
La Palma, 104
Laborem Exercens, 92
Ladino, 28
Lake of Nicaragua, 113
Land to the tiller program, 106
Laos, 106
Laviana, Father Gaspar Garcia, 48
Lebanon, 112
legalism, 1, 60
Leo XIII, Pope, 7
Liga Campesina (Guatemala), 27
Limbo, 23
low-cost housing, 112
Luther, Martin, 2

Mangurian, David, 4
Maruzzo, Father Marco Tullo, 42
Marx, Karl, 7, 8, 17
Marxism, 3, 4, 5, 6, 7, 15, 16
  Marxist-Christian dialogue, 2

Mary, 109
Maryknoll, 2, 14, 57, 60, 61, 63, 64,
  69, 70, 105
  seminary, 74
Mater et Magistra, 2
McCormack, Father John J., M.M.,
  69
Medellin (Colombia), 6, 71
Mein, John Gordon, 60
Melville, Father Art, 68, 70
Melville, Father Tom, 68, 70
Mexican/French declaration, 104
Mexico, 57, 106, 113
Michaelangelo, 11
Milan, 11
military buget in U.S., 115
minimum guaranteed income, 110
Miskitos, 33
moral perfectionism, 112
Morelos, Father, 19
Motagua River, 29
Mujahadeen, 88
Mullahs, 86, 88
mythology, 115

Nagasaki, 89, 114
National Catholic News Service, 69
National Council of Churches, 64
National Council of Resistance
  (Iran), 87
National Guard (U.S.), 6, 49
National Liberation Front
  (Vietnam), 105
National University of Guatemala,
  66
Nazis, 59
Nebaj, 99
nerve gas, 115
New Exodus, 77
New International Economic
  Order, 103, 111
New Testament, 67
New York City, 114
New York Times, 15
Nicaragua, 3, 10, 11, 12, 15, 17, 33,
  84, 91, 106, 111, 112, 113, 115
Ngo Dinh Diem, General, 105
Nobel Prize, 110
North Vietnam, 106
Norway, 106, 113